Cambridge Elements

Elements in the History and Politics of Fascism
edited by
Federico Finchelstein
The New School for Social Research
António Costa Pinto
University of Lisbon

THE RISE OF MASS PARTIES, LIBERAL ITALY, AND THE FASCIST DAWN (1919–1924)

Goffredo Adinolfi
University Institute of Lisbon

Shaftesbury Road, Cambridge CB2 8EA, United Kingdom

One Liberty Plaza, 20th Floor, New York, NY 10006, USA

477 Williamstown Road, Port Melbourne, VIC 3207, Australia

314–321, 3rd Floor, Plot 3, Splendor Forum, Jasola District Centre, New Delhi – 110025, India

103 Penang Road, #05–06/07, Visioncrest Commercial, Singapore 238467

Cambridge University Press is part of Cambridge University Press & Assessment, a department of the University of Cambridge.

We share the University's mission to contribute to society through the pursuit of education, learning and research at the highest international levels of excellence.

www.cambridge.org
Information on this title: www.cambridge.org/9781009564410

DOI: 10.1017/9781009564366

© Goffredo Adinolfi 2025

This publication is in copyright. Subject to statutory exception and to the provisions of relevant collective licensing agreements, no reproduction of any part may take place without the written permission of Cambridge University Press & Assessment.

When citing this work, please include a reference to the DOI 10.1017/9781009564366

First published 2025

A catalogue record for this publication is available from the British Library

ISBN 978-1-009-56441-0 Hardback
ISBN 978-1-009-56439-7 Paperback
ISSN 2977-0416 (online)
ISSN 2977-0408 (print)

Cambridge University Press & Assessment has no responsibility for the persistence or accuracy of URLs for external or third-party internet websites referred to in this publication and does not guarantee that any content on such websites is, or will remain, accurate or appropriate.

For EU product safety concerns, contact us at Calle de José Abascal, 56, 1°, 28003 Madrid, Spain, or email eugpsr@cambridge.org.

The Rise of Mass Parties, Liberal Italy, and the Fascist Dawn (1919–1924)

Elements in the History and Politics of Fascism

DOI: 10.1017/9781009564366
First published online: February 2025

Goffredo Adinolfi
University Institute of Lisbon

Author for correspondence: Goffredo Adinolfi, Gbgai@iscte-iul.pt

Abstract: Through an in-depth study of the electoral process, the aim of this Element is to analyse the political transformations that occurred in Italy from 1919 to 1924. After the takeover of the lower house by the mass integration parties in 1919 – Popular and Socialist – concerns grew within the liberal camp. The argument of this Element is that the conservatives failed to adapt and remain competitive in a system characterised by universal suffrage, thereby paving the way for the rise of the fascists. The electoral path to power begins with the political elections of 1921, continues through the renewal of the municipal councils in 1922–3, and concludes with the elections of 1924 when Mussolini managed to take control of the low chamber. The Duce assumed the role of head of the nation, presenting a list of candidates – the Listone – that included members of the Fascist Party and the former political elite.

Keywords: fascism, democratisation, elections, mass parties, liberal Italy

© Goffredo Adinolfi 2025

ISBNs: 9781009564410 (HB), 9781009564397 (PB), 9781009564366 (OC)
ISSNs: 2977-0416 (online), 2977-0408 (print)

Contents

Introduction	1
1 The November 1919 Elections	5
2 Local Elections and the Bologna Clashes: The Rise of Paramilitary Influence	25
3 From the 1921 Elections to Mussolini as President	40
4 The 1924 Elections	59
Conclusion	77
References	83

Introduction

This Element aims to analyse the transition of the Kingdom of Italy towards a democracy based on mass integration parties and the events immediately preceding its transformation into an authoritarian regime. This topic has been tackled in millions of pages, generating extensive and diverse literature. In my opinion, however, the topic has not yet reached a definitive conclusion and it is one upon which the scholarly community is far from agreement. This Element, therefore, certainly does not set out to put an end to a debate of this magnitude but intends to make a very specific contribution to it, based on just two dimensions: an electoral and, to a lesser extent, institutional analysis. The period between 1919 and 1924 marks a critical transition phase from ongoing democratisation to its collapse and the onset of an authoritarian shift. The analysis specifically focuses on the electoral cycles that initiated this transition in 1919, when the Popular Party (Partito Popolare) and the Italian Socialist Party (Partito Socialista Italiano) secured a majority in the lower house. This critical juncture represents a decisive crossroads, where the clash between different political visions led to the rise of Benito Mussolini. As will be demonstrated in the Element, an epilogue that initially was neither foreseeable by any of the actors involved nor, obviously, inevitable.

The Italian Political System in the Aftermath of the First World War

At the turn of the twentieth century, the Italian political system had been democratising, amidst ups and downs and gradually, but at a relatively steady pace. Since 1861, when the newly constituted Kingdom of Italy inherited the Statuto Albertino (Albertine Statute) as a constitution from the Kingdom of Sardinia, the spheres of participation had gradually widened to include growing numbers of citizens. One of the high points of this process was the approval of the 'almost' universal suffrage in 1912 for elections to the Chamber of Deputies, the only elective chamber. The 1913 elections that followed had produced a transformation that was still largely silent and not fully perceived by most. As Alessandro Schiavi (1914) reported, however, the dichotomy then ceased to be between liberal, conservative, and progressive forces but between liberal forces and Socialists, at that time the only party with a mass, national structure. The events of 1915 that led to the country's entry into the First World War, on the other hand, showed how its democratic foundations were still fragile and how, from within the country, a new social class was emerging that opposed the Socialists and parliamentarism and reverted to hyper-nationalist logic. With Italy not yet involved in the First

World War, after the street demonstrations of the 'Radiant Days of May', the Chamber of Deputies, with a neutral majority, was therefore forced to accept a fait accompli and approve the state of war, something that took place on the basis of a double pressure: on the one hand, that of the movement that aggregated various very violent interventionist forces – nationalists, D'Annunzians, and Mussolinians – and, on the other, the Crown itself and the conservative liberals who were at the head of the government. Once the war was over, a long phase of institutional fluidity opened in Italy and Europe. In a sign of great instability and the search for a new order, five electoral cycles followed one after the other, from 1919 to 1924: the legislative elections of 1919, 1921 and 1924 and the administrative elections of 1920 and 1922–3. This transition initially seemed to lead to a completion of the democratisation process and only later ended with the consolidation of an authoritarian regime. In this Element we shall focus on this period, in order to understand the electoral and institutional dynamics that allowed the transition from the first to the second part. And, to do so, we shall focus, above all, on the relationship within an imaginary triangle formed by representation, the parties, and elections. Within this triangle, the focus will be on analysing the cleavage opposing liberal formations to mass integration parties and, even more specifically, on the attempts to construct a conservative party capable of integrating the middle classes within democratic institutions. This process was particularly significant because it was a response to the evolution of the Socialist Party, which had already completed its process of affirmation and integration of the proletarian classes, both urban and agricultural.

It was necessary to adopt a multilevel approach in order to understand the deeper reasons for this long process of transformation. The First World War and its consequences on society were certainly among the causes that accelerated a process that was already underway, but behind them laid implicit dynamics, associated with the transformations that preceded the war, and explicit ones: that is, referable to the political system, such as the suffrage reform approved in 1912. The first level lay in the paradox of a democratisation process that would remain partial and unfinished and that, in fact, would never touch the Albertine Statute granted in 1848. Akin to what happened in other European countries after the First World War, a broad debate developed in Italian public opinion, in the parties and among constitutionals, which focused, above all, on the need for reform of the Senate, the upper chamber that, although not elective, retained numerous powers to intervene in the legislative process. In addition, the discussion addressed the issue of the multiple powers that the king still exclusively enjoyed, particularly in the field of foreign policy. The convocation of a constituent assembly, which could have overturned the relationship between the Crown and the representative institutions, was then also hypothesised. Whereas under the statute these were still in some way legitimised by the king by their very existence, with the constituent assembly it would be the king who would be legitimised by them, as had happened for example in Belgium, where the sovereign had been chosen by the assembly after the approval of the constitution in 1831. A paradigm shift that was not easy to accept in the House of Savoy because, although the action in the political system of the heads of state had often been silent, it was far from irrelevant (Colombo, 2010: 10–15). In this context, the elections of 1919 represented the greatest upheaval in Italian politics since the beginning of the liberal age. The mass parties then became a majority in the Chamber of Deputies, while the upper chamber maintained a majority of 'Constitutionals'. The shock brought about a substantial freezing of the debate on the reformability of the political system and an accentuation of a desire for crystallisation that would preserve it from complete disruption.

The second level was the crisis of all the political formations and the upheaval of previous balances. In the conservative camp, there was a real crisis and the inability of the right-wing leadership to adapt to the new rules imposed by the enlargement of suffrage. This made it difficult for part of the country to identify with the democratic state. The inability to constitute a viable party proposal in this field was undoubtedly partially due to the fact that a large section of the liberal world would have preferred a return to a model in which the government was not dependent on the confidence of parliament, instead returning completely to the sphere of the king; that is, they wanted a 'return to the Statute' – a more rigid interpretation of the constitutional charter. Added to this was a second dimension that upset the balance of the political system, namely the birth of a Catholic party. In 1913, in the first elections with universal male suffrage, the Catholic vote had united to support the candidates of the liberal formations. In 1919, on the other hand, Catholics stood as candidates with their own party, the Popular Party, which obtained 20 per cent of the seats in the lower house, inevitably causing a haemorrhage of votes, especially in the north, for the Constitutionals. However, the party that soon showed an intrinsic weakness, due to the contrast between different currents, some more intransigent and others more attentive to collaboration with the conservatives, and the fluctuating relations with the Vatican. Finally, there was always the seemingly unstoppable development of the socialist movement and the workers' movement: socialists who were also internally far from united and who would soon go through the split from the left of the future Communist Party and the marginalisation of the reformists.

Some Methodological Notes

Before proceeding, it seems useful to clarify some relevant methodological notes. Firstly, it is necessary to define the typology of the parties involved, aiming to reduce complexity, number, and diversity, even if at the cost of some precision. They will be grouped into two broad areas, liberal parties and mass integration parties. Liberal formations – or formations of cadres or notables – will be defined as all those formations with little or no formalised organisational structure, not dependent on a membership base, generally composed of social, economic, and intellectual elites and with that privileged negotiation between elites. Here, given the impossibility of reconstructing the extremely chaotic and volatile field of liberal parties (Democratic, Liberal, Constitutional, etc.), they will be grouped together in a dimension that, following a cataloguing model proposed by the Ministero dell'economia (1924a: 55), joins all these formations under the single definition of *Costituzionali* (Constitutional parties). On the other side of the spectrum, there were the mass integration parties. For the sake of simplicity of analysis, here we will define a mass integration party on the basis of three dimensions. The first is the organisational structure, that is, they have an organisation rooted in the territory based on militancy. The second is the mobilisation strategy: that is, they aim to mobilise broad sectors of society, often around ideologies or collective identities. The third is the relationship with voters. That is, they seek to create direct and lasting ties with their voters, often through the offer of material and symbolic benefits and through building 'party loyalty' among their members and supporters (Duverger, 1954: 63–78).

The second methodological note concerns the data considered and processed. Electoral statistics, an impressive mass of numbers, allow us to understand in depth the political balances and imbalances in their evolution. It was decided as a starting point to recount all the candidates and all those elected in all the electoral rounds considered, starting from the tables compiled at the time by the official bodies and not referring to secondary sources. Unfortunately, reading them is not always easy: the geography of the constituencies changed from election to election and so it was necessary, in order to favour comparability, to reduce their complexity. An attempt was therefore made to convert the constituency map to a single geographical scheme, summarised not on the province but on the region, or in some cases on an amalgamation of regions. The analysis of the electoral data was done by emphasising four cleavages that seemed the most effective for understanding the critical juncture: north/south, abstention/participation, local/legislative elections, and mass/constitutional parties. A separate discourse will be made for the selection of candidates for the 1924 Fascist List and elections. In this case, it was necessary to focus more on the precise reconstruction of the biographical data of each of the individual candidates in order to bring out the relationship and transition between the old elites and the new elites.

Finally, we chose to focus on a rereading, also from the primary sources, of the main newspapers of the time. Many newspapers were consulted, but we chose to favour the detailed analysis of the liberal-leaning *Corriere della Sera*, the Italian newspaper with the largest circulation of the time. Its pages are essential to understand the climate and to grasp the point of view of those who considered themselves on the side of the ruling class and how the transition process to a democracy based on mass parties was experienced.

Inevitably, there was not space in this Element even for many relevant things. We wanted to focus almost exclusively on the electoral processes. Thus, it was impossible – and probably would not have been consistent with the specific approach chosen for this study – to delve into the events linked to the Biennio Rosso (1919–20) or Gabriele D'Annunzio's adventure in Fiume (1919–20). This is not so much because their importance and destabilising effects are not understood but because an attempt will be made here to identify the weaknesses of the Italian political system, even in what appears less visible. Thus, the events surrounding the March on Rome are only dealt with in terms of the negotiations for the formation of a new government between 27 and 30 October. We will not dwell too much on the violence of squadrism, except when it has a direct impact on institutions, such as when the assault on the municipal chambers led to their dissolution. These are all issues that have been abundantly addressed and resolved elsewhere.

1 The November 1919 Elections

The Popular Party

The 1913 elections had not ended in catastrophe for the parties of the liberal sphere only because the Catholics, not yet organised into their own autonomous party, had supported anti-socialist candidates on the basis of a specific programme. In 1919, however, Catholics entered the political arena themselves, organising themselves into a nationwide structured party, the Popular Party, founded on 18 January 1919 by the parish priest Don Luigi Sturzo, with the appeal 'To all free and strong men'. It was a party that was already born with a number of peculiarities. First of all, it was born out of the coming together of many and very different Catholic organisations. Then, since its birth, it had formed itself an organisation similar to that of the Socialist Party which, since 1892, the year of its foundation, had branched out into a dense network of parallel structures, such as trade unions and cooperatives. The birth of the

Popular Party also called into question the clear separation of Church and State and Pope Benedict XV's revocation in 1919 of the *Non expedit*, or Vatican ban on Catholics taking part in national votes, a separation that had been maintained since the taking of Rome in 1870, when Italian troops put an end to the existence of the Church State. The party, therefore, was not born out of nothing: it could already count, at its inception, on the Catholics' mature experience in parliament and government. They had managed to gather nineteen deputies in the group, and by the time of the Bologna Congress in the summer it had grown to thirty-one.

For our analysis, it is important to emphasise the effect that the birth of the Popular Party had on both the party system and the political system. On the face of it, the Popular Party was a force that at times appeared parallel and specular to the Socialist Party, sharing in part its structure and its corporatist/democratic afflatus: that is, the desire to overcome the capitalist economy (De Rosa, 1972: 24), and the demand for the transformation of the Senate. They shared, in other words, everything that Italian liberalism had always tried to avoid. In the Popular Party programme, there were three points that concerned a broad transformation of representation: the electoral law, which was to provide for proportional counting and also the proposal to grant women the right to vote; the administrative decentralisation of municipalities, provinces, and regions; and the electivity of the Senate, with the introduction of corporatist principles (Cantono, 1920).

After the challenge of the Socialist Party which, in 1913, had already obtained almost 20 per cent of the votes at a national level, concentrated mainly in the north of the country, the liberal world was now also challenged in its waning hegemony by the entry on the scene of another mass integration party that was competing for the favour of contiguous sections of the electorate. In 1913, in a system made up of uninominal constituencies, the liberals, thanks to the Gentiloni agreement, had been able to save themselves thanks to the Catholic votes, that support was now lacking (Adinolfi, 2024: 36). Sturzo, moreover, had not looked favourably on that agreement and believed, on the contrary, that the involvement of Catholics should be carried out in the first place with an autonomous force. Even the new Pope Benedict XV had shown himself benevolent towards Sturzo's initiative and, although he never openly expressed his support, this did not seem to be enough to limit the dissension in the Catholic world and within the newly formed party. The currents that formed within it immediately undermined the party in depth and, as we shall see, played a crucial role in all the salient moments of the following years. It was thus configured as a party divided between an intransigent current, headed by its leader, and a 'collaborationist' one, closer to the more conservative fringes of the country. The centrifugal force exerted by these two currents, even in the face of a Holy See that was more inclined to support the collaborationist strategy, played a decisive role in causing the Catholic party project to collapse. Already in 1919, when Sturzo found himself having to construct lists for the elections, he felt obliged to take into consideration all the various souls of the party, from the clerical moderates to the nationalist Catholics. One of the first clashes came as early as 1920 over the formation of lists in the local elections, characterised by a majority law that had led to the aggregation of a poll whose only glue was anti-socialism (De Rosa, 1972: 97). Therefore, the Popular Party suffered from being both a governmental force and a sort of anti-system party at the same time and was hindered by these divergences in its project to take a central role in the political scenario in a country that had always been profoundly anti-clerical.

Towards a Conservative Mass Party

At the appointment with modernity the conservatives presented themselves without adequate answers. This is a fundamental aspect of Italy in 1919: on the right of the political quadrant there was a lack of credible proposals for the electorate, and this fragility would play a fundamental role in the following years. The question of creating a conservative party had, in fact, been dragging on for decades, without an effective solution ever having been found.[1] Since the 1911 war against the Ottoman Empire to gain control over Libya, nationalist ideals had enjoyed some success among students and the middle classes (Nardi and Gentili, 2009), and the idea of forming a Fascio Liberale,[2] a bloc to unify the conservative and liberal forces, began to make headway. The government crisis that followed the defeat at Caporetto in 1917 led to the presidency of the council by Vittorio Emanuele Orlando and the formation of a new group in the chamber that took the name of the Fascio Parlamentare di Difesa Nazionale (Parliamentary Fascio of National Defence). Initially, the Parliamentary Fascio was not intended as a party, but as an aggregation of parliamentarians of multiple political sensitivities with the sole purpose of supporting the new government in the context of the war. However, some MPs soon decided to give the new formation a permanent character, seeking to give it both a ramified organisation and a unitary statute binding on all members. The group, which met at a conference in Milan in early 1918, already counted on 158 deputies and

---

[1] *Corriere della Sera*, 7 April (1914).
[2] At the beginning of the twentieth century in Italy, the term *fascio* was frequently employed to signify the need for political parties or people to come together or unite. This usage highlighted a widespread sentiment towards unity and collective action within the political landscape of the time.

122 senators in May. The mass integration model aimed to bring together not only individual militants but also associations that could gravitate around the future party.

Yet, despite the conventions, conferences, and proclamations, the whole project struggled to take off as a structured party. On 25 May at the Argentina theatre in Rome, the Parliamentary Fascio, meeting with 300 associations, decided to give itself a unitary and federative structure.[3] On 20 November, it was Antonio Salandra who emphasised the importance of the new formation, given that 'great bold reforms were needed and it was necessary above all that the nation's supreme representatives could no longer be manipulated in an old church' and that 'the Fascios needed to survive the war'. On 21 January 1919, a more detailed programme came out calling for the vote for women and the demand for reform of the Senate. The experience of the Parliamentary Fascio, however, was soon shattered, overwhelmed by the very logic of that old world to which many of its adherents belonged: that of a policy based on old patterns and dialectics anchored to liberal dynamics, which saw the electoral constituency as a sort of possession of the deputy himself and, as such, not subject to party dynamics. The ultimate crisis began when the Fascio decided, on 14 July, to vote against the Nitti government:[4] a wrong that was never forgiven.

Despite its short duration, the significance of the Fascio's experience was remarkable both for the Italian political system as a whole and for the history of the organisation of liberalism. A significance rooted first of all in its numerical size and in the fact that the organisation was able to embrace both the chamber and the Senate and, further still, in the discipline required and the subordination of individual parliamentarians. And, finally, in how, once the war was over, it was able to exercise a degree of control over the Orlando government that would have been hardly conceivable in the pre-war parliamentary context (Ulrich, 1996: 497). With its failure, the possibility of rebalancing the Italian party system, orphaned of a conservative right wing capable of aggregating an important part of society, was also definitively closed, making available, to those capable of occupying it, all the political space left unoccupied by the contraction of the Liberals.

Senate Reform

The transformations of the political system had never touched the Albertine Statute: the major reforms of those years had only concerned suffrage and electoral law. The practice, however, had changed considerably: generally, the

---

[3] 'Salandra's speech', *Corriere della Sera*, 21 November (1918).
[4] 'Il Fascio', *Corriere della Sera*, 4 October (1919).

executive depended on the confidence of parliament. However, it should not be forgotten that the House of Savoy, at crucial moments, could and did use its powers, as had happened in 1915 with the First World War (Colombo, 2010). To these de facto transformations, a series of profound transformations in the party system, as seen so far, had been added, generating an anomalous situation in the functioning of parliament. Until 1913, the majorities in the Senate and the Chamber of Deputies were largely consistent, not least because senators were appointed in large groups. This was due to 'waves of appointments' proposed by the government and accepted by the king. The Senate's approval of what had already been discussed in the chamber was not at all taken for granted, and it also had a conditioning effect. The measures were generally negotiated between the two branches of parliament. In a mass integration-party system that emerged from the 1919 elections, however, this mechanism generated different majorities in the two branches of parliament that blocked the political decision-making process. The elections had highlighted a major contradiction that had hitherto mattered little: the problem of the non-electivity of the Senate.

After all, even at a European level, the transformations taking place were profound, and all went in the direction of greater democratisation. The problem of the 'constituent assembly', that is, of an elective chamber with the task of drawing up a new fundamental charter, was firmly in the background of the debate at the time as the reform of the Senate. An article by Senator Tommaso Tittoni (1918), published in the pages of *Nuova Antologia*, offers insight into some of the proposed reforms that were being considered at the time: a Senate term of nine or twelve years with partial renewal to ensure continuity of the office; reduction of the royal appointment to a limited number of senators, creating an electoral college made up of universities and high culture associations; and second-tier regional election. Outside the Senate, the ideas in this regard were obviously much more radical. As early as February 1919, Claudio Treves, a socialist deputy from the reformist faction, advocated for the need for a constitutional assembly to review the entire institutional framework and to abolish a Senate that was 'the powerful reserve army for supporting the will of the king and the ruling political class against the will of the people'.[5] The Popular Party also recognised that the state's crisis was a crisis of its institutional form, and that this crisis concerned, above all, the lifelong assembly (Lanciotti, 1993: 300). However, the Catholics' idea was to establish an elective Senate as a direct representation of national, academic, administrative, and trade union bodies, offering an alternative model to both the socialist and liberal models. The former was based on the idea of class, and the latter was based on

---

[5] *Critica Sociale*, 3, 1–15 February (1919), 2.

individualism. The popular model, on the other hand, provided for a strong organic inspiration (Antonietti, 1985: 260).

The senators tried to survive in what was becoming a hostile environment for them. They discussed a reform that, in reality, failed to inspire enthusiasm among both the advocates of popular sovereignty and those of a political body that, in the liberal tradition, was supposed to defend the institutions from the very idea of that sovereignty. To study how to introduce elective elements into the upper chamber, a twenty-five-member commission was established. One of its proposals was to create a specific electoral constituency for the Senate, characterised by an electoral body distinct from that of the House. In August, the Senate reform bill was submitted to the offices. The bill proposed that the upper chamber would consist of 60 members appointed for life by the king, 60 elected by the Senate, 60 elected by the Chamber of Deputies, and 180 elected by constituencies. The commission largely favoured the introduction of an elective element, with only a minority opposing it, seeking instead to significantly limit the scope of this reform. The majority report justified the reform with the need to establish criteria of popular sovereignty to the second branch of parliament, a representation that had to be of both voters and interests. In this sense, therefore, the new Senate was to incorporate the principles of representation and, at the same time, counterbalance the Chamber of Deputies, which, with universal suffrage, became a chamber representing the interests of the majority classes of society, that is, the lower classes. Hence the need for its reform in order to remedy this paradox.

Changing the direction of these debates came with the November 1919 elections and the affirmation in the Chamber of Deputies of the Socialist Party – with 156 deputies – and the Popular Party with 100 (256 out of 508). The political climate altered abruptly and the Senate became the bastion of defence for the liberal political class.

Electoral Law Reform

In April 1918, the government had extended the parliament elected in 1913 by one year and, after a series of relatively complex steps between the chamber and Senate, on 16 December 1918, the right to vote was extended to all male citizens aged twenty-one and older (Ballini, 2011: 4). In March 1919, socialist leader Filippo Turati proposed a proportional electoral reform to the chamber. The underlying idea of the reform project was to channel anti-system or opposition forces within the institutions (Ballini, 2011: 6). The proposal for the new law was accepted, but not with the broad agreement that had characterised the approval of the 'almost' universal suffrage in 1912. At the time,

Giuseppe Micheli, a Catholic member of parliament, clarified that the proposed electoral law wouldn't merely entail transitioning from a single-member constituency system to a proportional one; rather, it would signify a shift towards acknowledging the party-based system of representation. In short, the concept of mass party representation was to 'overcome the inorganic and apolitical atomism of electoral localism' (Ballini, 2011: 10). In the end, the proportional reform aggregated 240 votes in favour and 63 against, thus becoming Law No. 1401 of 9 August 1919. Consequently, the constituencies were redefined in September. The 508 deputies of the new parliament were to be elected in 54 constituencies, consisting of one or more provinces. Moreover, there was no reward for political forces that were organised at a national level to reduce fragmentation. In this way, forces that had a strong local base in the constituency were favoured.

The number of deputies to be elected in each constituency varied from 5 to 20 (Figure 1) and the size of the constituencies ranged from 355,868 inhabitants in Caltanissetta to almost 2 million in Milan (Figure 2) (Ministero per l'Industria, 1920: 20).

The average number of votes needed to elect a deputy thus varied considerably from constituency to constituency: in Potenza, 47,969 voters were sufficient; in Rome almost 100,000.

As shown in Figure 3, it was an extremely diverse electoral geography, which generally favoured proportionality. Few deputies were elected in small districts, which, given the D'Hondt method, tended to favour larger parties.

The Socialist Party between Social Democracy and Communism

The events occurring within the Italian Socialist Party at that time reflected the challenges, trends, and uncertainties of the European left. First of all, it must be specified that when we refer to *socialists* we must think of a complex universe, made up of multiple organisations that coexisted and were intertwined with each other. There was the trade union of the Confederazione Generale del Lavoro (General Confederation of Labour – CGdL), there were the cooperatives, the taverns, the party, and the Case del Popolo (People's Houses). Then there were the municipal administrations, with which, through the municipalities, public services were implemented; from welfare, such as kindergartens, to the electrification and development of public transport. The socialists had given life to a project that was as much political as existential and which was constituted, through its network, by a totalising experience, transversal to the public and private spheres of the people who militated in it. The party had

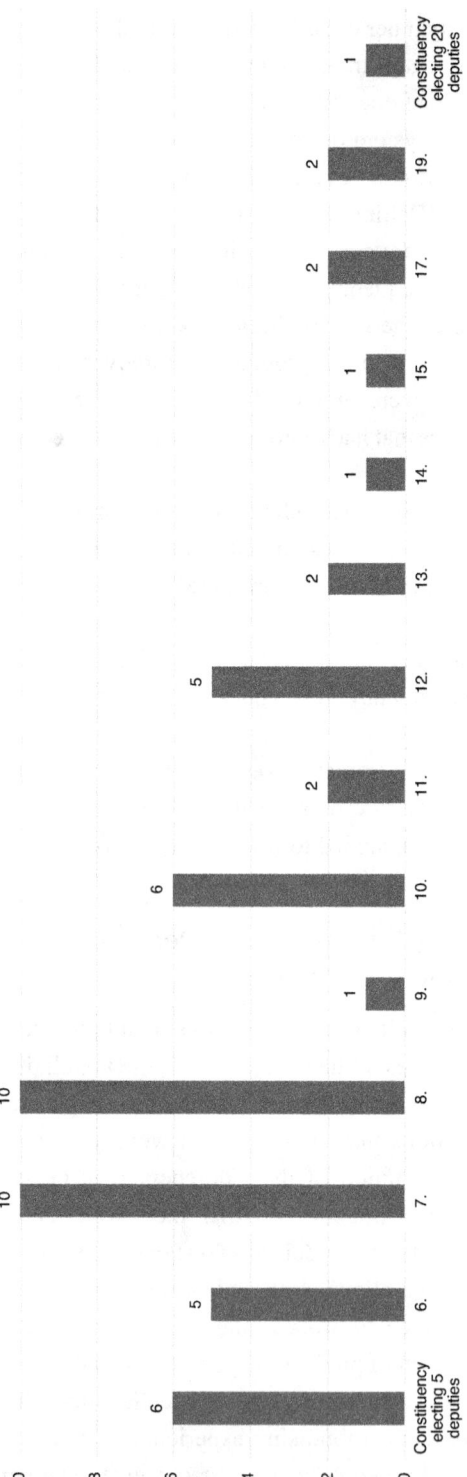

Figure 1 Number of deputies elected in each constituency.

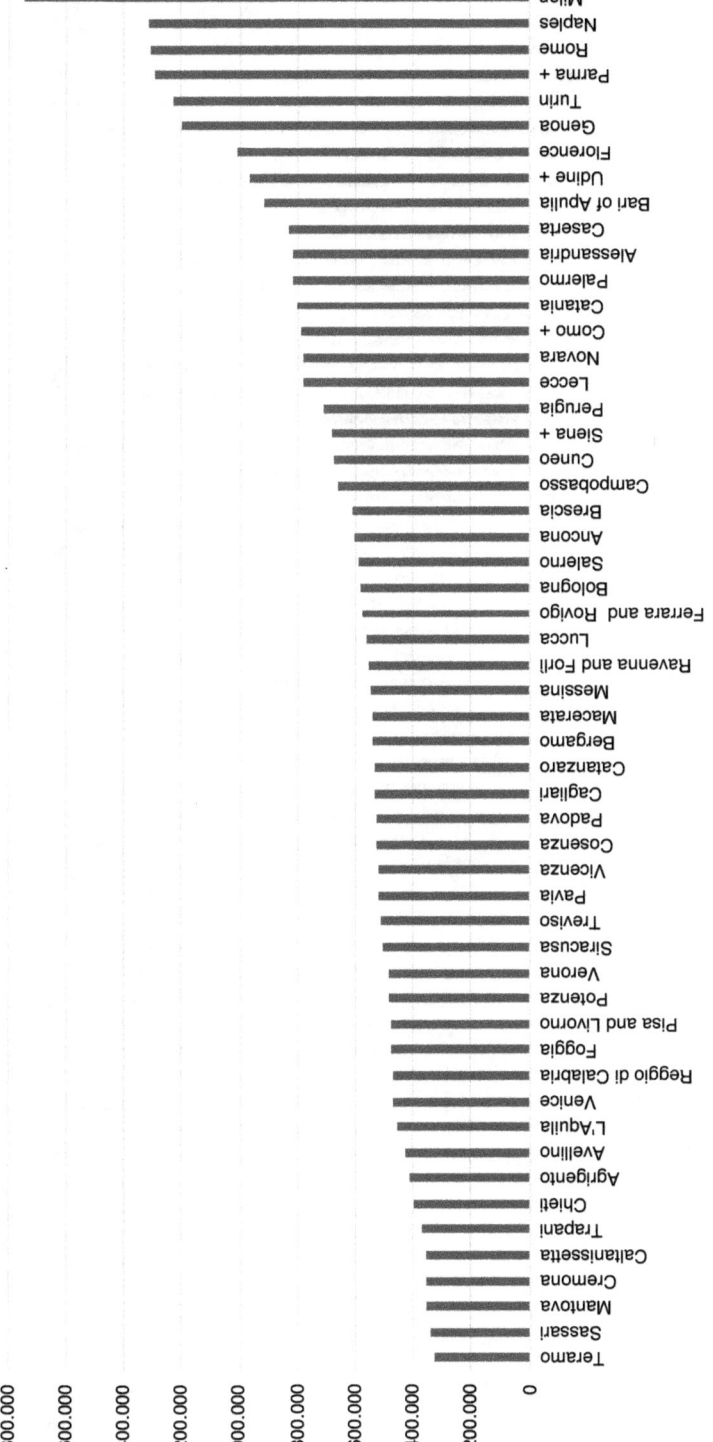

Figure 2 Number of inhabitants in each of the constituencies.

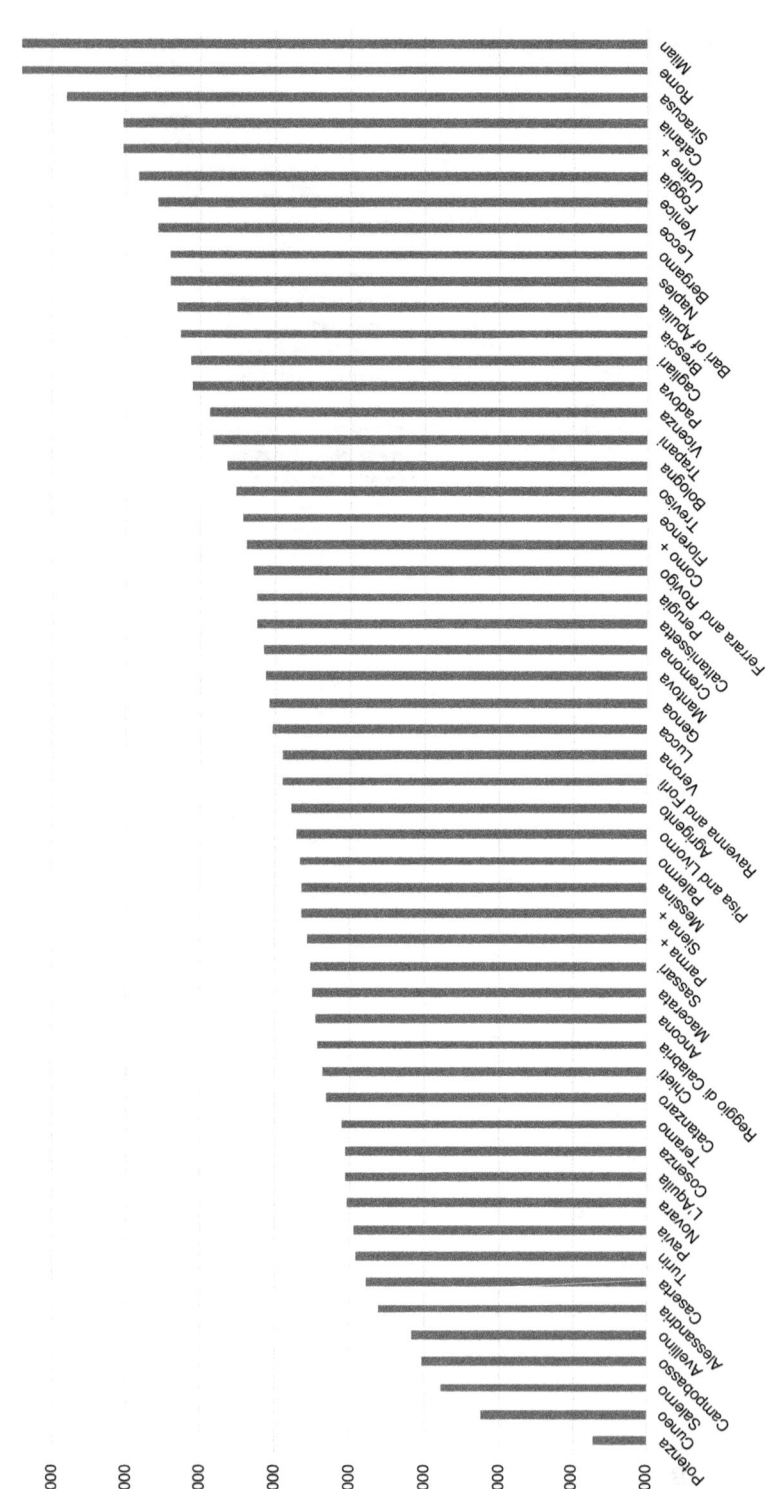

Figure 3 Electors needed to elect a deputy.

developed mainly in Emilia, Tuscany, Veneto, Lombardy, and Piedmont, but had not managed to cross the borders of the south. Among the larger European socialist parties, it had also been the only one to maintain a neutralist position throughout the First World War and had paid the price with the arrest of many of its leaders, including its own Secretary Costantino Lazzari and Giacinto Menotti Serrati. Despite the electoral weight and the fact that they had played a fundamental role in democratisation processes, the socialists had never held government roles except at the level of municipal administrations. Finally, it had been thanks to a sort of alliance between the Liberal leader Giovanni Giolitti and Turati that, in 1912, the reform that led to 'almost' universal male suffrage had been approved. But, in the post-war period, these *informal collaborations* were no longer tenable, and positions had become decidedly polarised.

It was inevitable then that, in a framework where the conflict had not lived up to the promises made on the eve of the conflict, the legitimacy of the socialists was very high. A further inevitability was that, after the Soviet Revolution and with the terrible economic conditions that followed the war, tensions within the party would grow and pressure from below, which had manifested itself in the spontaneous bread riots in Turin in August 1917, would increase (Arfé, 1975: 251). At the XVI Congress in Bologna in October 1919, the party decided to join the Third International, or Communist International, by acclamation – a choice that had also arisen as a consequence of the collapse of the Socialist International that had preceded the world conflict through the Brussels International Bureau. The relationship with Moscow, with all its contradictions, would then characterise the entire life of the socialists in the post-war period. In contrast to other European experiences, the Italian Socialist Party housed both revolutionary and reformist factions, with the revolutionary faction itself divided into communists and socialist maximalists. In 1919, most of the revolutionary movements outside Russia had been quashed. Despite the persistence of revolutionary rhetoric, few were truly convinced that the Bolshevik revolution was imminent. Theoretically, there was a proposal to replicate what was done in Russia. Still, in practice, it became evident that such a course of action was unfeasible. It was evident to most that the state was, in any case, stronger and much better organised in the field of repression. Membership of the International implied the acceptance of a number of rules, including that of expelling the reformist fraction. On this point, the party wavered, and the breakaway of the Reformists only came in October 1922, in a climate already deeply marked by fascist violence and just days before what was to be the March on Rome. Until then, however, some form of coexistence between the two factions of the party, albeit with increasing conflict, was always found, and the split came not from the reformist side but from the communist faction at the

Livorno Congress in January 1921. In the aftermath of the 1919 Congress, however, it was still possible to celebrate the unity of the party and start campaigning for elections.[6]

The 1919 Elections: The Electoral Earthquake

On the eve of the 1919 election, predictions made by the *Corriere della Sera* seemed to reassure liberal circles of the turnout results. The general forecasts gave the Socialists between 90 and 100 seats – a third of which to the maximalists – and the Popular Party between 65 and 75. The *Costituzionali* would, therefore, be left with 350 of the 508 seats, a more than sufficient portion to be able to govern. Thus, it was predicted that 30 per cent of seats would go to the mass parties and the rest to a plethora of undefined, divided formations, unable to build stable majorities.[7] Before proceeding to an analysis of the results of 1919, it must also be remembered that, in the 1913 elections, the Socialists had taken almost a million votes, about 17 per cent, but, penalised by the single-member electoral system, only fifty-two deputies.

Taking a very first look at the structure of the results coming in from the polling stations (Table 1), there were just over 10 million registered voters, from which, however, had to be subtracted the emigrants, some 500,000, and the soldiers who were not entitled to vote; almost 1 million.[8] Participation was low: about 60 per cent of the eligible voters had voted, less than in 1913. The turnout was very high in Emilia (71 per cent), followed by Lombardy, Piedmont, and Tuscany. In contrast, the turnout was very low in Sicily (50 per cent), Campania, and Marche. In general, more people voted in the northern regions than in the south. There was also very high fragmentation. On average, ten lists were presented for each constituency. The highest number was in Campania, with twenty-one lists, and Sicily with fourteen. Lazio and Umbria and Marche, on the other hand, had six and five lists. Only two lists were present in almost all the constituencies: the Socialist and Popular lists. The re-election rate of the deputies who were already in the chamber in 1913 was very low: in 1919, 65 per cent of those elected became deputies for the first time; by far the highest figure ever. This proportion had, in fact, been 32 per cent in 1913 and even 21.3 per cent in 1900. Only the southern regions had slightly lower percentages of newly elected representatives, but they were still over 50 per cent (the only exceptions being Abruzzi and Molise, where it was 45 per cent) – an anomalous

---

[6] *Avanti!*, 24 October (1919). [7] *Corriere della Sera*, 16 November (1919).
[8] The results of the 1919 elections were rearranged on the basis of the 1924 constituencies, so fifty-four were reduced to fourteen; the one in Venezia Giulia did not yet exist.

Table 1 Results of the 1919 Italian parliamentary elections

Regions	Average Voters	N. Lists	Electorate	Emigrants	Soldiers	Voters	Valid Votes	Socialists N.	%	Popular Party N.	%	Costituzionali N.	%	Other N.	%
Piedmont	66.0%	11	1,130,418	43,430	79,324	665,388	646,396	326,574	50.5%	122,927	19.0%	196,895	30.5%		
Liguria	61.2%	8	403,575	8,966	49,105	211,428	211,428	66,529	31.5%	42,913	20.3%	101,986	48.2%		
Lombardy	67.3%	11	1,484,105	22,745	140,942	889,178	889,178	409,389	46.0%	268,473	30.2%	211,316	23.8%		
Veneto	57.6%	10	1,121,219	26,107	112,204	566,432	555,032	207,642	37.4%	186,653	33.6%	150,243	27.1%	10,495	1.9%
New Provinces															
Emilia	70.8%	8	811,912	11,738	103,813	492,688	490,693	288,194	58.7%	92,643	18.9%	83,093	16.9%	26,764	5.4%
Tuscany	62.5%	10	895,186	23,355	109,907	476,289	473,543	207,791	43.9%	94,298	19.9%	156,333	33.0%	15,121	3.2%
Marche	50.7%	5	367,619	24,612	33,704	156,879	154,976	52,143	33.6%	42,380	27.3%	48,205	31.1%	12,248	7.8%
Lazio and Umbria	54.6%	6	632,301	42,673	40,137	300,112	295,506	99,358	33.6%	66,323	22.4%	108,745	36.8%	21,080	7.0%
Abruzzo and Molise	57.7%	11	582,882	80,628	27,002	274,249	277,492	28,729	10.4%	20,044	7.2%	228,719	82.4%		
Campania	51.1%	21	962,445	48,607	37,943	447,371	444,500	26,586	6.0%	81,995	18.4%	305,984	68.8%	29,935	6.7%
Apulia	55.4%	9	648,483	23,153	43,844	322,155	322,173	59,015	18.3%	33,758	10.5%	229,260	71.2%	140	0.0%
Calabria and Basilicata	55.9%	12	622,773	82,169	25,103	288,216	286,920	19,196	6.7%	37,317	13.0%	228,653	79.7%	1,754	0.6%
Sicily	49.8%	14	1,165,775	83,934	65,817	505,919	498,812	32,682	6.6%	62,075	12.4%	398,544	79.9%	5,511	1.1%
Sardinia	56.0%	9	244,421	4,607	11,197	127,957	127,588	10,964	8.6%	15,556	12.2%	101,068	79.2%		
Total	59.2%	10	11,073,114	526,724	880,041	5,724,261	5,674,237	1,834,792	32.3%	1,167,354	20.6%	2,302,818	40.6%	369,273	6.5%

Table 2 Deputies elected in 1919 elections.

Regions	N. of deputies	Newly elected MPs	Re-elected MPs	Average newly elected	Socialists		Popular Party		Costituzionali		Other		Percentage mass integration parties
					N.	%	N.	%	N.	%	N.	%	
Piedmont	56	37	18	67	29	51.8%	11	19.6%	16	28.6%			71.4%
Liguria	17	12	5	71	6	35.3%	4	23.5%	5	29.4%	2	11.8%	58.8%
Lombardy	64	39	21	65	31	48.4%	20	31.3%	12	18.8%	1	1.6%	79.7%
Veneto	46	30	15	67	18	39.1%	17	37.0%	10	21.7%	1	2.2%	76.1%
New Provinces													
Emilia	43	25	18	58	29	67.4%	7	16.3%	5	11.6%	2	4.7%	83.7%
Tuscany	39	27	12	69	18	46.2%	8	20.5%	10	25.6%	3	7.7%	66.7%
Marche	17	12	5	71	6	35.3%	4	23.5%	6	35.3%	1	5.9%	58.8%
Lazio and Umbria	25	16	8	67	9	36.0%	5	20.0%	10	40.0%	1	4.0%	56.0%
Abruzzo and Molise	29	13	16	45	3	10.3%	1	3.4%	23	79.3%	2	6.9%	13.8%
Campania	47	27	20	57	2	4.3%	10	21.3%	34	72.3%	1	2.1%	25.5%
Apulia	28	15	13	54	5	17.9%	2	7.1%	17	60.7%	4	14.3%	25.0%

Calabria and Basilicata	33	18	15	55		4	12.1%	28	84.8%	1	3.0%	12.1%
Sicily	52	26	26	50		6	11.5%	42	80.8%	4	7.7%	11.5%
Sardinia	12	7	5	58		1	8.3%	10	83.3%	1	8.3%	8.3%
Total	**508**	**304**	**197**	**65**	**156**	**30.7%**	**100**	**19.7%**	**228**	**44.9%**	**24**	**4.7%**	**50.4%**

figure that broke all averages and gives us a first indication of what was happening.

On 18 November 1919, *La Stampa*, the liberal daily newspaper based in Turin, commented on the election results with a full-page headline: 'The resounding condemnation of the war in the suffrage of the people. The enormous socialist dominance and the affirmation of the Popular Party'. In essence, the electorate's condemnation of what had been an unwanted intervention that had generated immense drama was unequivocal.[9]

Indeed, the Socialists, the most determined anti-war political force, were by far the most voted-for party, with almost two million votes and 32 per cent of the future parliament, followed by the Popular Party with just over one million votes (20 per cent). The mass parties obtained more than half of the votes, with 156 and 100 seats respectively (Table 2), that is, an absolute majority of the 508 deputies in the chamber. The Fascio Parlamentare elected only two deputies, Paolo Boselli and Giuseppe Bevione, but it must be said that it did not even present itself with its own list, but rather joined those of the Monarchist Liberal Party (Baravelli, 2021: 278). The figures, of course, varied from region to region. For instance, the Socialists failed to secure any Calabria, Basilicata, Sicily, and Sardinia deputies. However, they constituted the majority in Piedmont. Moreover, in Emilia, they boasted a significant representation of 67 per cent of the deputies. The Popular Party was also decidedly stronger in the north, where it had 31 per cent in Lombardy and 37 per cent in Veneto, while in the south, it only obtained percentages between 10 and 20 per cent in all constituencies (Table 2). In other words, the mass integration parties established their influence across all economically advanced regions characterised by rapidly changing social structures. The results of the Constitutional parties were specular to the Socialist and Popular: they were in the minority everywhere in the north (around 20 per cent), while in the south, from Abruzzo downwards, they were everywhere above 80 per cent. Italy still remained a strongly divided country, with polarised political, economic, cultural, and social structures clearly visible in the election results. The defeat of the Fasci di Combattimento, Mussolini's party, was also harsh: its results clearly showed that it was still extremely fragile and that, as Renzo De Felice points out, the figure of 40,000 members propagated in the election campaign had been greatly inflated (De Felice, 1965: 568). They also lacked a precise strategy of alliances because, on the one hand, Mussolini imagined making blocs with left-wing interventionism; on the other hand, Michele Bianchi was more inclined to settle on a case-by-case basis (De Felice, 1965: 569). In this scenario, the conflict

---

[9] See *La Stampa* and *Corriere della Sera*, 18 November (1919).

between the mass integration parties and the liberal parties became increasingly bitter and it was soon realised that there would be no way to proceed to a synthesis: it would require the defeat of one of the two sides. While the socialist leadership decided to protest as early as the traditional inauguration of the king's legislature, the anti-socialist voices coming from the press became threatening.[10] Treves already sensed, from those first warnings, that the socialists had become in everyone's eyes the force to be eradicated by any means and that revolutionary rhetoric would end up backfiring on the party itself.[11] The *Corriere della Sera* called for a breakaway of the reformist wing of the official Socialist Party, to which, according to the Milanese daily, a clear alternative was opening up: on the one hand the Russian or Hungarian example and, on the other, the German or Austrian example. Thus, from many quarters, pressure was beginning to mount on Turati for a split in the reformist wing of the party, which, as we have seen, would not happen until much later.[12] However, the *Corriere della Sera* also underlined the inability of the liberal parties to mobilise their electorate. They considered the defeat of the liberal camp without appeal, caused by the inability to respond to discontent and face peace negotiations. In the meantime, the Popular Party presented itself as an alternative pole of attraction for all anti-socialist forces, also aiming to gather the sympathies of those who saw the need to oppose the nationalist tendencies and violence growing in those months.

The Revolution of the Mass Parties

Figure 4 shows the distribution of deputies by geographical area. Thus, there is a dual cleavage – geographic and partisan – which overlap. In the north, the combined total of deputies from the Popular Party and the Socialist Party represents 76 per cent, against a national average of 50 per cent. In the south, deputies from the constitutional forces still constitute a very substantial majority (61 per cent). Another potentially alarming fact is that socialists in the north account for 50 per cent of the total.

The division between mass integration parties and liberals transcends mere formalities. These two spheres embody entirely different perspectives on representation. The newly emerged mass integration parties are characterised by an internal cohesion that, compared to the fluidity of the Liberals, appears uncompromising. The negotiation processes within the lower house, which were prevalent in the pre-war period, were essentially flexible. Even

---

[10] *Corriere della Sera*, 29 November (1919).
[11] *Corriere della Sera*, 20 November and 4 December (1919).
[12] *Corriere della Sera*, 19 November (1919).

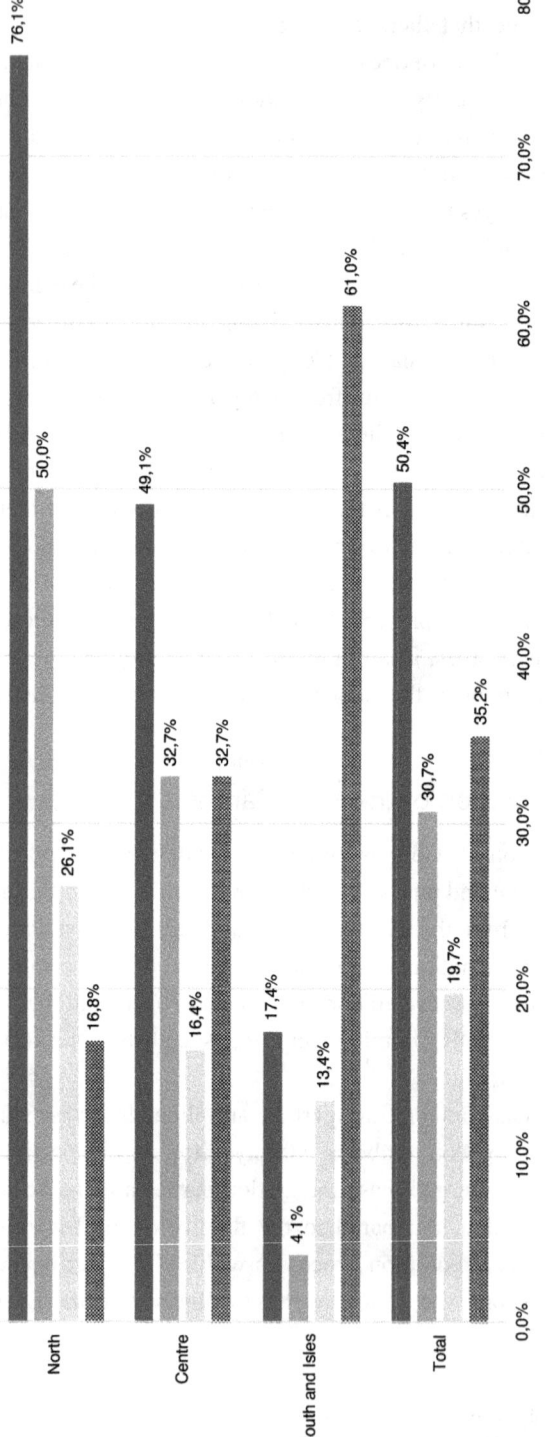

Figure 4 Mass integration parties (Socialist and Popular) versus *Costituzionali* parties (north, centre, south), 1919.

amidst profound ideological disparities, the liberal objective was always to amalgamate the necessary forces to reach a consensus.

Moreover, parties lacking a national organisational structure and extensive grassroots militancy for vote gathering within a context shaped by universal suffrage and mass integration found it imperative to professionalise to remain competitive (Offerlé, 1999: 105–10). The contemporaries had already discerned, upon analysing the reasons for the defeat, that it was not merely a matter concerning a single party but encompassed the entirety of the liberal system itself.[13] That is, there was already an awareness among commentators and political actors of the time that a system of unrecognisable formations, assembled differently constituency by constituency, without an ideology or an identifiable programme, made the chances of victory very reduced. The Liberals accused the proportional system of having led to a situation of ungovernability but, in reality, in some ways, it had lessened their defeat. The crisis of legitimacy among the ruling classes, as manifested in the electoral outcomes, was further exacerbated by the shift from a single-member constituency, which emphasised individual candidates, to a proportional system that prioritised party representation (Leoni, 2001: 390).

However, it would be overly simplistic to confine ourselves to this explanation. Furthermore, as we have seen, the adopted proportional electoral system did not provide any national-level reward. Each of the fifty-four constituencies had its dynamics, symbols, and alliances, which varied significantly from one another. This allowed local notables to maintain significant control over their constituencies, as they still viewed them as their own. As a result, they felt little need to align with a more organised entity across the entire country. Senator Francesco Ruffini, in the face of this seismic event, saw the non-elective Senate as a chamber that had a function of discipline and orientation, but he also clearly recognised that a historical cycle had closed and that both the Senate and the Liberal Party would have to renew themselves profoundly. Gaspare Ambrosini – a constitutionalist – spoke explicitly of a new regime in which the old constitutional norms had passed away, having been replaced by the norms of the new constitutional system (Ambrosini, 1922). And, indeed, the consequences of the transformation on the way the political system functioned could be seen immediately. In fact, Sturzo proposed bargaining between the political groups for the formation of the government, which conditioned the Popular Party's participation in the government on the acceptance of specific non-negotiable programmatic points (De Rosa, 1972: 38), a proposal that Nitti immediately condemned, considering it detrimental to the constitutional

---

[13] Ministero per l'Industria, *Statistica delle elezioni generali*, p. 53.

traditions and the very rights of the Crown. It was evident that the liberal system, while partly understanding what was happening, was too sclerotic to react accordingly. As Ambrosini (1922: 198) explained, it was impossible for them not only to accept the new status quo but even to theorise the question of the transition from a model of cabinet government, in which the leader was appointed by the king, to parliamentary group government, in which the government formation was based on the decisions of different political groups. The king's appointment of the prime minister now had 'to follow new procedures, dealing impersonally with the leaders of the parliamentary groups' (Ambrosini, 1922: 187). The programme, the ministers, and the number of portfolios were negotiated with the parliamentary leaders. The already underway process will be further deepened with the reform of July–August 1920 when the Committees of the Chamber of Deputies takes on a permanent character (Orsina, 1996: 397). It was decided that they would be formed not by random selection but based on political groups and that they would have significantly greater power to oversee the government's activities (Ambrosini, 1922: 192).

An incomplete and highly contested transformation remained: it was as if there were two different and parallel systems in one country. The 1919 election marked a critical juncture in which two different political models clashed within the two countries, leading to a highly unstable political system (Istituto Centrale di Statistica, 1947: 131–2).[14] Amidst the significant transformation in the party system, one of the primary cleavages was the discrepancy between a lower house holding a majority and a Senate aligned with a different faction. With its appointive nature, the Senate appeared largely immune to the sweeping changes occurring within the political landscape. In a system of bicameralism, in which the lower house had greater powers in practice, but the upper chamber had the power to reject measures, a system incapable of functioning was created. The lower house was more supportive of measures proposed by governments led by Nitti or Giolitti, especially those aimed at increasing state intervention in the economy. However, this faced opposition from the Senate, posing a weakness the governments couldn't afford to ignore. In the months following the 1919 elections, the perception of the end of an era was clear to the main part of the political actors. It was understood from many quarters that a complete upheaval of the landscape was taking place, marking at the same time the rejection of an entire ruling class and of the political system itself. The popular and socialist parties were the bearers of an institutional project radically different from the

---

[14] In 1919, within the Senate, the mass integration parties, comprised 52 official socialists, 20 Catholics, and 9 conservative Catholics.

existing one. Whether the revolution was socialist or merely democratic or aimed at the convocation of a constituent assembly and the abolition of the Senate or its reform, it was equally unacceptable to part of the liberal world and the Crown.

2 Local Elections and the Bologna Clashes: The Rise of Paramilitary Influence

Transformations in the Representation of the Municipality

During the Italian democratisation process, the significant transformations at the local level played a pivotal role. Therefore, the local level is the fundamental observatory to comprehend the societal transformation process. The organisation of the relationship between the central state and the municipalities was inherited, at the unification of Italy, from the legislation of the Kingdom of Sardinia. Local administration was still regulated by a law from the pre-unification period of 1859 (Royal Decree No. 3,702 of 23 October 1859) which, along the lines of the French model, divided it into provinces, districts, mandates, and municipalities. Each province was headed by a governor, later named 'prefect' (Royal Decree No. 250 of 9 October 1861), who depended on the Ministry of the Interior, the instructions from which he had to execute. The municipal administration was then partially reformed by Law No. 2248 of 20 March 1865 which, however, kept intact all the highly restrictive criteria present in the previous legislation, both with respect to control by the central government and to the restriction of the census with regard to the electorate (Istituto Centrale di Statistica, 1947: 58).[15]

The municipality consisted of a municipal council, which served as the assembly, and a Giunta, which functioned as the executive branch. The municipal councils were responsible for the 'rules of the Charity and Charity Institutions' (Art. 82) and it was their task to deliberate 'the active and passive budget of the municipality, and that of the institutions belonging to it, for the following year' (Art. 84). They were 'subject to examination by the council the budgets and accounts of the administrations of parish churches and other administrations, when they receive subsidies from the municipality' (Art. 83). Municipal councillors were elected for five years, 20 per cent of whom were renewed each year. If municipal councillors are not re-elected, they cannot retain their position in the Giunta. The main organ, the mayor ('head of the municipal administration and officer of the government', Art. 97), was appointed by the king, who also had the power to dismiss him. The mayor,

---

[15] The number of citizens registered in the lists for the year 1887 was 2,026,619.

chosen from among the municipal councillors, remained in office for a period of three years and was confirmed if he retained the office of councillor (Art. 98).

The expenses of the municipalities were divided into compulsory and optional. The compulsory ones were clearly regulated and constituted a long list of competencies, which included, for example, street lighting or compulsory education. Nothing was specified with regard to optional expenditure (Art. 117), but the way in which this expenditure could be financed was detailed. Art. 118, reformed in 1870, stipulated that, in the event of insufficient revenues, the municipalities could levy duties on beverages and building materials, impose taxes on the occupation of public areas or on draught animals and even dogs; and establish surtaxes on direct contributions. In essence, therefore, an important first nucleus of the welfare state developed around the activity of the municipality, which could take advantage of having broad powers both in deciding which entities to finance and how to finance them, through extended powers even in terms of taxation.

In 1889, the Crispi government approved Royal Decree No. 5921 of 10 February that introduced profound changes in the relationship between the central state and the municipalities. The electivity of the mayor by the municipal council was introduced and the term of office was reformed, making it renewable for three years (Art. 123). Secondly, a limitation to four-fifths of councillors per list was introduced to ensure that minorities were also represented. The voting system provided for a complex mechanism, whereby the voter indicated a list of names he preferred, without any indication of party, and those candidates who had obtained the most votes were elected councillors. The partial renewal of one-fifth of the councillors each year was maintained (Art. 229). The new legislation regulated the mayor's removal process in detail. The highest representative of the municipality 'if he does not fulfil his obligations or does not fulfil them regularly' (Art. 52) or for 'serious reasons of public order, or when called upon to observe obligations imposed on them by law, they persist in violating them' (Art. 52) could be removed and temporarily replaced by the figure of the Commissioner.

Closing the cycle of a period of major reforms came Municipal and Provincial Electoral Law No. 640 of 19 June 1913, which extended universal male suffrage to administrative elections as well (Art. 28). The second article of the law contained another innovative element: it stipulated that the municipal and provincial councils, as well as the council and mayor, would remain in office for four years (revision of Art. 271) and that they would be fully renewed at the end of their term, abolishing the mechanism of partial renewal in order to give greater continuity to the administration. The counting of votes would remain as a majority, as was established in Law

No. 5921 of February 1889. In accordance with these legislative reforms, all municipal councils were then renewed (Art. 3).

The Municipality, the Welfare State, and Public Entrepreneurship

The necessity for municipalities to implement increasingly expensive public services imposes significant changes in their role. Initially, it was the practice to entrust private companies with the management of a wide range of these services, such as street lighting or the construction and operation of aqueducts and tramways. However, this model had begun to show signs of crisis due to the numerous conflicts of interest that arose and the fact that it generated increased profits for the entrepreneurs that did not translate into increased quality of these services. As a result, there had been a trend towards the direct takeover of public services by the municipal administration. This change had been facilitated by an expanded reading of Municipal and Provincial Law No. 164 of 4 May 1898, which gave municipalities the right to own property and establishments.

The municipal dimension, therefore, became fundamental for socialists, both because of the pedagogical character it assumed, thanks to the small size of the territories and the direct relationship with the citizens that could be established there, and because it represented the only possibility of accessing positions of effective government of an administration, since they were still precluded from participation at a national level (Degl'Innocenti, 1984: 5). The municipality, in other words, was the only place where executive functions were not strictly the prerogative of the liberal ruling classes. The municipality, then, also had other symbolic functions for socialists, including countering the centralism of power or developing a deeper idea of community (Ridolfi, 1992: 64). The history of the local government is in essence a parallel one, which developed thanks to the reform desired by Crispi and which saw Socialist representation spread like wildfire from 1889 onwards, when the 'Reds' decided to present themselves with their own candidates in many cities, sometimes alone and sometimes with other lists. On the other hand, the attainment of state power through the conquest of the municipalities, considered by the Socialists as the central pivot of their action and the first step of its extension, was part of the 'minimum programme' decided upon at the National Council of the Socialist Party meeting in Bologna in March 1895 and then ratified at the Rome Congress in 1900.[16]

The implementation of municipalised companies, useful for municipalities to increase their structure, arrived in Italy with a noticeable delay, compared to

---

[16] Art. 8, Partito Socialista Italiano, *Statuto, Programma Massimo e Minimo del Partito Socialista Italiano*, (Firenze: G. Nerbini, 1910), p. 13.

countries such as Belgium or Great Britain. At the beginning of 1900, the legislative framework within which to operate was not consistently defined: the Law of 20 March 1865 No. 2248 allowed municipalities to manage enterprises directly, as long as they had a general interest purpose. To completely change the relationship between municipalities and enterprises, Law No. 103 of 1903 came into effect, drawn up by Giovanni Montemartini and desired by Giolitti, which aimed to create a legislative framework in which municipalities could municipalise public services in a specifically regulated context. The exponential growth of cities, the need to 'electrify' and the need to develop transport and water services made it necessary to push the accelerator of development. Private entities had hitherto been reluctant to invest and innovate and, when they had done so, the costs were significantly higher than those of direct management. Many sectors were covered by the reform, from public transport to electricity production and distribution of telephones. The passing of the law gave rise to sharp contrasts, both in the chamber and, even more decisively, in the Senate, where it passed with a difference of only eighteen votes (eighty-five in favour and sixty-seven against). The Liberals considered municipalisation acceptable only if it was in areas of 'natural monopoly'; that is, where competition was not possible, and if it was to curb external contracting out to private companies in fields where there was a lot of investment.

The municipalised companies that had arisen as a result of this revision of the legislation were the responsibility of the municipal council, but they had a separate management structure, consisting of a director and an administrative commission. Article 13 of Law 103 also altered and innovated the system of representation, because it introduced the instrument of popular consultation (it was, in fact, a referendum, even if it was not so expressly defined) which implied a binary 'yes' or 'no' choice with regard to the resolutions of the municipal council. In order to understand the extent of the municipalisation process that took place in those years, it is useful to cite a study that came out at the same time as the law was passed by Riccardo Bachi, published in Luigi Einaudi's journal, *La Riforma Sociale*. It was a long, statistical study involving over a hundred Italian cities on the issue of municipalised companies. The services managed by the municipalities at the time were mostly those of the electricity network, sewers, aqueducts, and gasometers, but there also appeared, as in Reggio Emilia, a pharmacy to distribute medicines to the poor, bakeries for the production and distribution of bread, and workshops for the maintenance of plants, as had been decided in Milan (Bachi, 1903: 48–9). To understand the transversal nature of the support for this type of reform, we can cite the case of Rome. Here, Montemartini himself, elected to the municipal council with the socialists, joined the municipal administration led by Ernesto Nathan in 1907.

He then initiated a process of intense municipalisation, especially in the fields of electricity, social housing, and transport. To approve these projects, a popular referendum was called on 20 September 1909, in which all parties sided with the 'yes' vote, thus giving the consultation a foregone conclusion. There was a widespread feeling for the need to move towards an entrepreneurial municipality, driven by the large influx of people into urban centres and the need to contain their discontent. Suffice it to say that, in 1903, Schiavi (1911: 26), director of the Istituto Case Popolari (ICP) in Milan, wrote that 332,841 inhabitants (70 per cent of the population) occupied only 172,417 rooms, or an average of one room for two people. In Florence in 1907, 9,150 families lived in 6,673 dwellings. So, a few weeks after the approval of Law No. 103, Parliament also gave the go-ahead to the law wanted by Luigi Luzzatti to encourage the development and financing of social housing (Law No. 254 of 31 May 1903). The law combined the savings banks' need to invest with the need to build houses for the intermediate and weaker social classes. Within a short time, Istituti per le Case Popolari (Institutes for Social Housing) sprang up all over Italy and soon found themselves managing not only housing but also nurseries, libraries, and schools. While the Association of Italian Municipalities was born in 1901, promoting a more inclusive idea of the city, the Socialist communes organised themselves into provincial and national federations and leagues, with the objectives, set by the General Council of the League of Socialist Municipalities, of giving each other mutual support, defending their members, and coordinating action. The conquest of the municipal administrations by the Socialists was a phenomenon that grew exponentially over the years, also thanks to the reform that had enshrined the eligibility of the mayor. Thus, the Socialists began to play a leading role in local government, managing smaller administrations then, increasingly, larger cities; first in coalition with other forces of the so-called Extreme (an alliance formed by Radicals, Republicans and Socialists) and later on their own. In November 1889, Ugo Tamburini was elected as the first mayor to lead a socialist administration in Imola, thanks to a coalition united under the name Democratic League (De Maria, 2010: 81–7). However, the most important victory was in Rome, where Nathan, leading a Giunta formed by an alliance of radicals and socialists, served as mayor from 1907 to 1913. After the approval of universal suffrage in 1912 and with the strong affirmation of the Socialist Party in the local elections of 1914 – the first to occur after the approval of the new law – a strong paradigm shift took place. In this context, the greatest proponents of a municipalisation of services were the Socialist administrations, especially in Emilia, which made extensive use of the 1903 laws to expand the number of services under their control, and to meet the needs of their electoral base. And, thanks to the same law, where there was hesitation on the part of the Ministry of the Interior, which, through its municipalisation offices, supervised and limited the activities of the municipalities, the legitimisation of the popular referendum often intervened (D'Amuri, 2013: 250).

In 1914, the Socialists' strategy changed, abandoning coalitions to go it alone in the elections. In the 1914 electoral round, Socialist municipalities rose to 450 out of a total of 8,268, with a peak in Emilia where they accounted for 26.62 per cent of the total, followed by Piedmont, Lombardy, and Apulia at around 7 per cent (Ridolfi, 1992: 72). Then there was the crucial victory achieved in Milan, where the Socialists obtained 44.9 per cent (34,000 votes against 30,000 for the Liberals). Similar outcomes were seen in other cities, such as Bologna, where the Socialists won with 49.9 per cent (12,000 votes against the clerical moderates, who obtained 11,000) (Giusti, 1945: 56).

The 1920 Local Election Campaign

This long premise on the meaning and powers of the municipality in its dual function as local representative body and entrepreneur was necessary to understand the centrality of the 1920 local elections, which were held in a period of profound changes in the political balance. After the 1919 elections, it was clear to everyone that the north was at a high risk of falling completely into the hands of the two mass parties, the Socialists and the Popular Party. Moreover, those of 1920 were the first administrative elections after the First World War: the renewal of the municipal councils had been delayed and the scenario therefore saw 21 per cent of the municipalities governed by royal or prefectural commissioners and 40 per cent of the population administered by municipalities that had not been duly elected (Ministero per l'Industria, 1920: 50). These were highly polarised elections, held in a climate of great mobilisation and social clashes. Playing against the Socialists was the majoritarian electoral system, used to regulate the election of municipal representatives which, as we have seen, was still at that time inspired by logic unrelated to political parties; that is, it was a system in which the most popular candidates won, regardless of the proportion of their votes. It was a system that deeply damaged the Socialists, whose coalition power was in fact essentially nil. On the other hand, it was much easier in the municipal area to form large anti-socialist blocs, made up of liberals and Catholics who, contrary to the national level, had a long tradition of alliance in that dimension.

Therefore, at the core of these forces' campaign after the shock of the 1919 elections was the objective of consolidating all available resources to defeat the Socialists, leveraging the mechanisms of the majority electoral law. The

Socialist Party leadership, on the other hand, had decided that the line to be taken in the run-up to the administrative elections would be to govern the municipalities they held by aiming to solve the most heartfelt problems of social life, both through the use of the municipality as an instrument in itself and through the party's parallel organisations, such as cooperatives and People's Houses.[17] The Popular Party also decided to adopt the line of intransigence and thus partly breaking with tradition. The idea of the leadership linked to Don Sturzo was, on this occasion, not to ally with other political forces; a line that was not at all shared within a party that, as we have seen and will also see later, was divided internally between a more intransigent current linked to the social doctrine of the Church and a more conservative one, whose aim was to build anti-socialist coalitions with the liberals and linked to the so-called Newspaper Trust, led by the Count Giovanni Grosoli. The parliamentarians and ministers of the Popular Party were also for a broad alliance with the parties of order as they were defined by the *Corriere della Sera*,[18] especially as far as Rome was concerned, where it was suggested not to present a complete list of names so as to allow the liberal group to win more easily. Finally, even the Holy See seemed to be increasingly sceptical of Don Sturzo's political line and more favourable to a policy of blocs.

The same divisions were reproduced at the level of the local elections that had been present at the national level and which were both inter- and intra-party. There were in fact three blocs – Liberal, Socialist (divided into reformist and revolutionary) and Catholic – which in turn were divided internally and without any real synthesis being possible in at least two of the blocs. In the middle of the election campaign between 19 and 20 September 1920, Turati instead gathered the members of the party's reformist wing in Reggio Emilia. The line of the *Corriere della Sera*, again, was to favour a dialogue between the elements within the Popular Party and the Socialist Party, which were more willing to block against what it considered the two opposing extremes – socialist, on the one hand, and nationalist and/or fascist, on the other. Thus, it also gave Turati's reformist congress great emphasis, with headlines occupying its entire front page.[19] The ultimate hope, not even hidden, was that Turati and his current would leave the Socialist Party.

Also playing a role in the configuration of the electoral blocs in 1920 was a clear dimension of well-defined and mutually opposing social classes. In the blocs of liberal formations, not only political organisations but also class or category organisations came together. This strategy, of course,

---

[17] *Corriere della Sera*, 3 September (1920).   [18] *Corriere della Sera*, 5 September (1920).
[19] 'The vote of the centrist socialists in Reggio against Bolshevism and for the conquest of power', *Corriere della Sera*, 13 October (1920).

also took into account the results of the political elections of 1919, and turned the local elections into a pronouncement that was experienced as an attempt to redeem the liberal and conservative world. Thus, for example in Turin, the Popular Party decided to be part of the 'constitutional blocs' because, looking at the results of the 1919 political elections, it was a city in the balance between conservatives and 'Reds'. In Rome, the Blocco di concertazione was joined by both the Camera dell'impiego pubblico, the trade union institution that brought together public administration employees, and the Associazione dei combattenti. In Milan, the Blocco di azione e di difesa sociale list brought together almost the entire non-socialist world: in addition to the 'constitutional' political groups, there were the nationalists, industrialists, and a whole series of organisations linked to the middle class, from doctors to the Federal Chamber for Public Employment to shopkeepers. In Milan, but on the socialist front, the maximalists reached an agreement with the socialist centrists.

In comparison, there were in fact two different and irreconcilable models of interpreting the municipality: one, that of the socialists, who wanted to develop a plan to finance social services, and the other, that of the constitutionals formations, careful not to raise taxes and not to overstretch the municipality's spending and interference.

The 1920 Elections, the National Blocs, and the Experiences of the Socialist Municipalities

The local elections of the autumn of 1920 constitute a sort of hinge between the phase of the Socialist Party's rise and that of its decline. Those elections, in fact, marked both the high point of a course that had begun at the end of the nineteenth century and the beginning of its decline (Degl'Innocenti, 1984: 12). On the socialist side there were high expectations of that electoral round, so a big leap was expected compared to 1914, when the last local elections had been held. On the other side of the political spectrum, the elections of 1920 marked the first attempt to form a bloc of agreement between Constitutionals, Popular Party, and Fascists with a purely anti-socialist aim (De Felice, 1965: 288).

Under the new electoral law (no. 1495 of September 2, 1919), all males who had reached the age of twenty-one by May 31 of that year were included on the administrative lists for 1920. Overall, the turnout at the national level was around 54 per cent, lower than the 59 per cent in the legislative elections in 1919. This is, however, an average figure that does not capture the large differences within the various municipalities (Figure 5). Therefore, in order to get a realistic picture of the situation, it is necessary to look at the details of certain realities on a case-by-case basis which, due to their importance, took on a more symbolic character than others. In Bologna, for example, participation fell from 63 per cent to 57 per cent. In some cities, such as Catania, it barely reached 20 per cent; in others, such as Milan or Turin, it was well over 60 per cent.

The constitutional parties (Table 3), obtained the majority of councils in 4,665 municipalities (56 per cent); the Socialists in 2,022 (24 per cent) and the Popular Party in 1,613 (19 per cent). In the provincial elections, the balance was more or less similar: Constitutionalists 33 (47 per cent); Socialists 26 (37 per cent), and Popular Party 10 (14 per cent) (Ministero per l'Industria, 1920: 60). However, the results here also varied greatly from north to south, as was already evident from the results of the 1919 legislative elections. The Socialists had a majority in 28 per cent of the municipalities in Piedmont, 32 per cent in Lombardy, 26 per cent in Veneto, 52 per cent in Tuscany, and 65 per cent in Emilia. On the opposite side of the peninsula, Campania and Sardinia saw Socialist administrations formed in less than 3 per cent of municipalities, in Calabria and Sicily in less than 9 per cent. By the 1920 elections, Socialists governed a quarter of the municipalities. The difference between 1914 and 1920 in local institutions was exponential and the Socialists went from a hundred or so administrations in Piedmont to 463, in Lombardy from 150 to 651, in Veneto from 31 to 220, in Emilia from 84 to 217 and in Tuscany from 12 to 154. Overall, however, constitutional formations prevailed in the large cities: that is, in Rome, Turin, Genoa, Florence, Naples, and Bari.

To understand the mobilisation capacity of the various forces, it is also essential to take a look at the electoral participation in certain constituencies. In Rome, the electorate grew from 47 per cent in the 1919 elections to 53 per cent in the administrative elections (Figure 5). *Corriere della Sera* celebrated the victory of the Constitutionals in this city with a full-page title. The margin between the formations was very wide: 40,000 votes for the union of the conservative formations, 20,000 for the Socialists, and 16,000 for the Popular Party. This meant, in the eyes of the commentators, that the conservatives had finally managed to mobilise their electorate, unlike in the 1919 legislative elections, as the *Corriere della Sera* itself had observed at the time. Although the Socialists in the capital had no ambitions of victory (and in fact they collected a percentage in line with the results of the 1919 election, when in the Lazio constituency they had obtained 25 per cent), the success of the bloc of the constitutional formations was hailed as a significant indicator of the growth of the conservative ability to mobilise broader segments of the electorate.[20] The results in Milan then became a kind of benchmark to assess the dynamics of the elections. Here, too, participation grew significantly, from

---

[20] 'Rome's electoral victory', *Corriere della Sera*, 2 November (1920).

Table 3 Number of municipal councillors elected in 1920 elections.

Region	N. electorate registered electors	N. electorate eligible to vote	Voters	Average voters	Costituzionali	Populars	Socialists	Republicans	Total	Socialists (%)	Populars (%)	Sum (Socialist and Popular)
Piedmont	1,279,425	1,244,091	740,665	59.53%	856	208	424	1	1489	28.48%	13.97%	42.44%
Liguria	448,676	429,825	234,130	54.47%	184	70	49		303	16.17%	23.10%	39.27%
Lombardy	1,598,537	1,545,288	998,753	64.63%	706	580	617		1903	32.42%	30.48%	62.90%
Veneto	1,173,890	1,122,234	632,921	56.40%	252	333	211	1	797	26.47%	41.78%	68.26%
New Provinces												
Emilia	917,650	884,927	526,673	59.52%	55	48	215	11	329	65.35%	14.59%	79.94%
Tuscany	940,568	902,844	503,134	55.73%	80	54	151	5	290	52.07%	18.62%	70.69%
Marche	383,646	370,196	169,086	45.67%	123	63	62	6	254	24.41%	24.80%	49.21%
Lazio and Umbria	684,312	658,099	372,016	56.53%	223	52	102	3	380	26.84%	13.68%	40.53%
Abruzzo and Molise	533,627	523,219	259,824	49.66%	406	9	45		460	9.78%	1.96%	11.74%
Campania	1,108,645	1,081,648	563,455	52.09%	537	68	18		623	2.89%	10.91%	13.80%
Apulia	695,346	677,730	372,005	54.89%	193	6	42		241	17.43%	2.49%	19.92%
Calabria and Basilicata	655,364	636,935	303,552	47.66%	463	33	45		541	8.32%	6.10%	14.42%
Sicily	1,276,057	1,252,702	543,333	43.37%	279	46	31		356	8.71%	12.92%	21.63%
Sardinia	255,013	244,931	135,210	55.20%	308	43	10		361	2.77%	11.91%	14.68%
Total	11,950,756	11,574,699	6,354,757	54.90%	4665	1613	2022	27	8327	24.28%	19.37%	43.65%

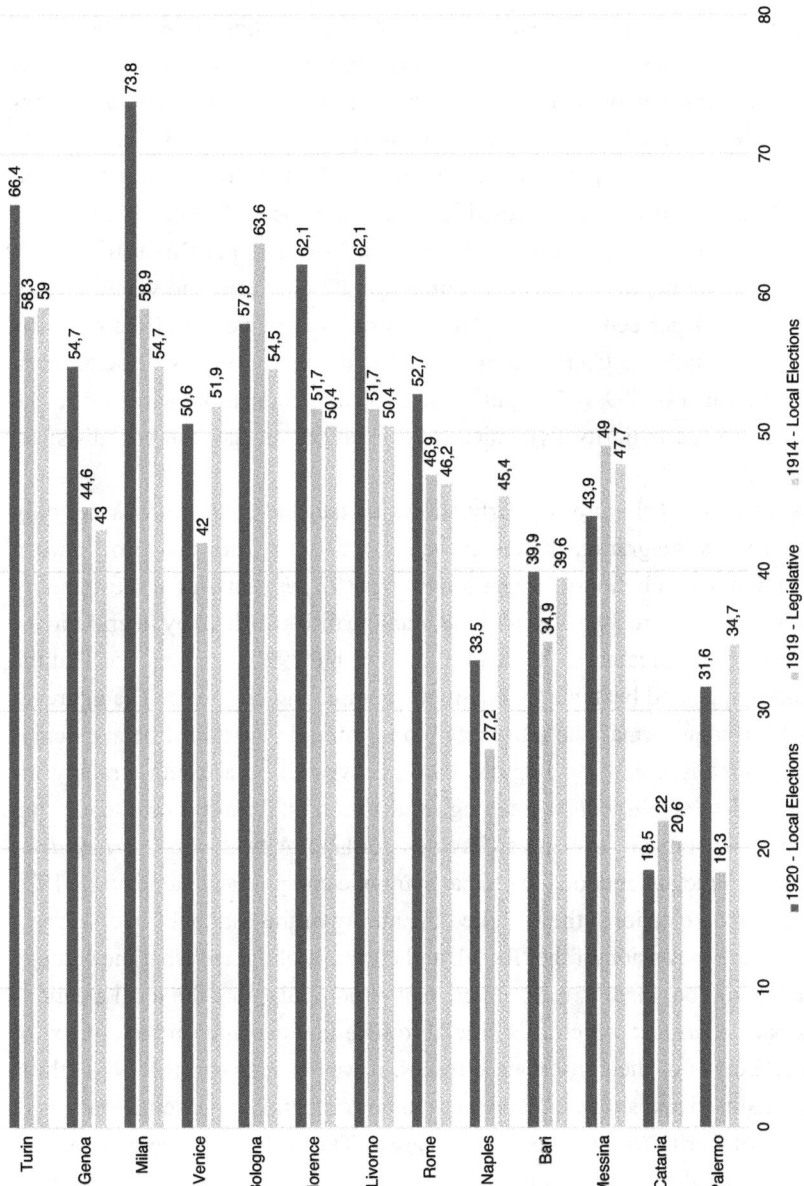

Figure 5 Participation in the 1914 municipal elections; 1919 legislative elections; and 1920 municipal elections (%).

59 per cent to 73 per cent (Figure 5). In 1919 the Socialists had obtained 54 per cent of the votes there and, in 1920, they won again, but by a narrow margin: they obtained just over 72,000 votes, compared to the 69,000 of the constitutional formations.[21] The figures are eloquent, because in the 1919 elections the Socialists had outnumbered the Constitutionals by 8,500 votes, in the local elections by only 3,000. However, the socialist Angelo Filippetti became the new mayor (Perazzoli, 2022: 134). In Turin came the most unexpected defeat for the Socialists, who, from the pages of the *Avanti!*, had already announced victory.[22] In the 1919 elections, 221,064 voters out of around 400,000 registered voters had voted in the constituency, of whom 116,000 had voted for the Socialists (just over 50 per cent) (Ministero per l'Industria, 1920: 126). Looking only at the Turin constituency, 58.3 per cent had voted there in 1919 and 66.4 per cent in 1920. The total number of voters in the city was 98,295. Although the Constitutionals prevailed slightly over the Socialists in absolute terms (48,899 votes against 48,575), the councillors assigned to the bloc, due to the majority dynamic, were many more than the socialists: 62 against 18.[23]

Just as in 1919, Figure 6 clearly shows us that the cleavage was not only between mass integration parties and constitutional parties but also between a north dominated by mass integration parties (57 per cent) and a substantially resistant south where 84 per cent of the municipalities are held by liberal forces.

Despite these successes, the central point of the 1920 elections was that the Socialists appeared beatable by coalitions comprising all forces. The aggregation of different formations into large blocs, bringing together liberals, democrats, nationalists, and the Popular Party, proved to be a useful strategy for defeating the Socialists and achieving results such as, for example, the election of a Nationalist mayor in Venice, Davide Giordano. Already the *Corriere della Sera* of the time understood the crucial symbolic and political value of the 1920 administrative elections: they marked the ability of the national forces to react and stem the expansion of the 'Reds', and clearly highlighted what the strategy to win should be. Finally, there is one fact in particular that the local elections bring back to us and which it is crucial to take into account: in the context of a general crisis of the conservative forces, it was then shown that when these were organised and showed themselves to be competitive, participation – as in the case of Turin, Milan, and Rome – grew. The widespread perception was therefore that if they managed to create a candidacy capable of attracting the conservative electorate, the chances of victory would also increase.

---

[21] *Corriere della Sera*, 9 November (1920). [22] *Avanti!*, 8 November (1920).
[23] 'The bloc's victory in the election of the Turin town council', *La Stampa*, 10 November (1920).

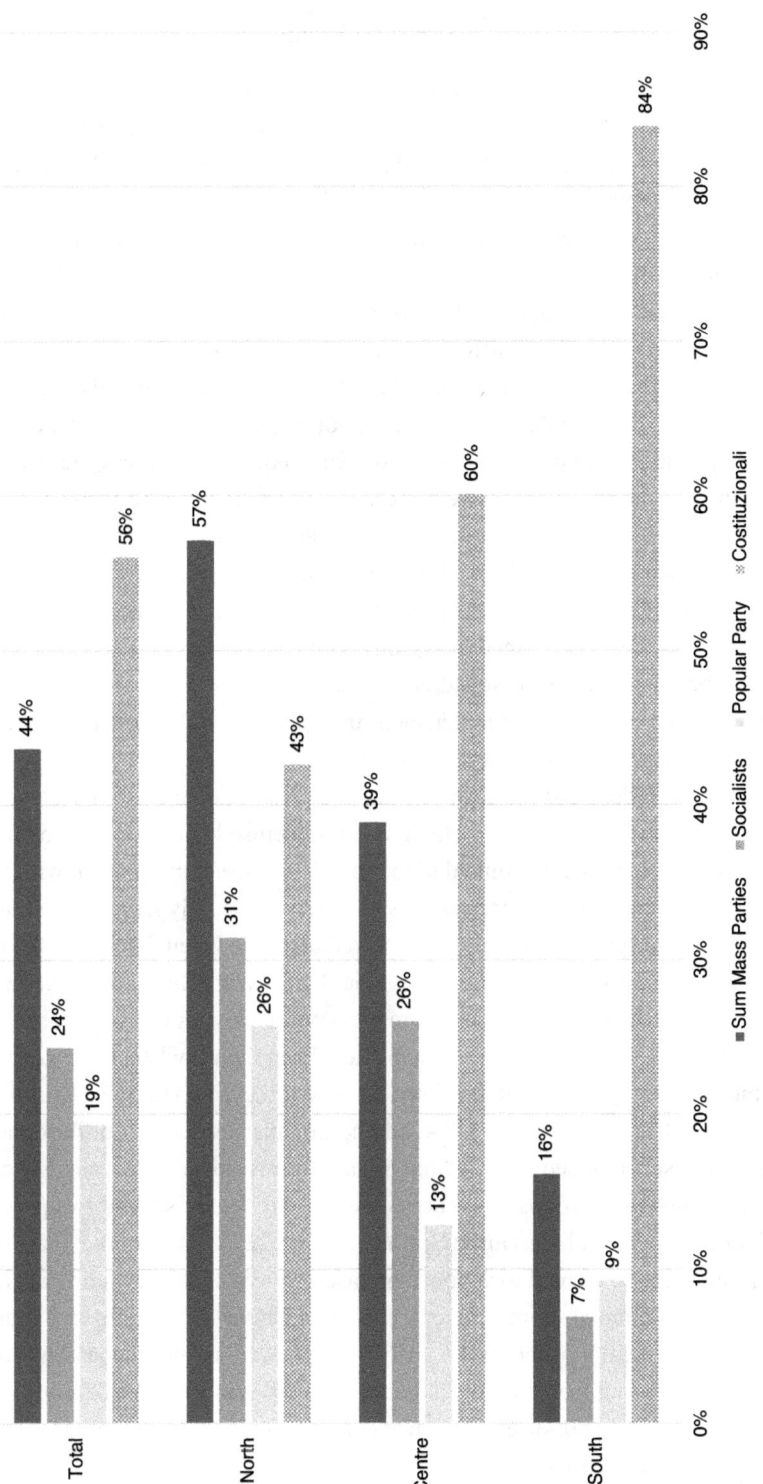

Figure 6 Local elections mass parties versus *Costituzionali* (north, centre, south).

Squadrism as a Form to Erase Socialism

In the elections of 1920, it was clearly shown how not only the creation of large electoral coalitions but also violence was considered a legitimate means to counter the rise of the 'Reds'. The socialist affirmation of 1919 was the starting point of the anti-democratic reaction, and in a few months, more than 500 local administrators was forced to resign due to the violence inflicted by the fascist squads (Ridolfi, 1992: 79).

Figure 7 shows the relationship between those arrested or denounced in 1921 among the squadrists and the difference in voting results between the 1919 and 1924 elections. The compilation of the data on which the graph is based depended on the will of the prefect (De Felice, 1966: 35–6; Saija, 2001: 367–8), who could decide almost autonomously when and how energetically to repress the fascist phenomenon. Therefore, the answers the chart gives us must be viewed with caution but they are, in any case, indicative of the general trend of the phenomenon. In other words, the graph shows how there was a connection between areas with a high socialist settlement and the arrest of *squadristi*. It indicates a strong correlation between the presence of regions with a strong Socialist Party settlement and the phenomenon of squadrism. This may not seem surprising, but it must be emphasised in order to understand future dynamics and how this correlation will influence the very essence of fascism.

However, to understand the strongly anti-socialist nature of fascist violence, it is necessary to take a step back. The first striking episode of the violent nature of fascism towards structures linked to the socialist movement is coeval with its very birth: the attack on the headquarters of the socialist daily *Avanti!* in Milan in March 1919; a symbolic event that occurred at a time when fascism still had a radically different form from the one it would later take. The *squadrismo* had developed robustly immediately after the great phase of workers' and peasants' mobilisation of 1919–20, the so-called 'Red Biennium', when Giolitti was presiding over the government and Bonomi was at the War Ministry. This was an important detail because, in 1924, the communist leader and philosopher Antonio Gramsci launched against Bonomi, a reformist socialist, the accusation of having transferred troops from active service to fascist squads to oppose socialism in Emilia and Tuscany (Gramsci, 1973: 227). The rumour that the Ministry of War had wanted to support the fascist movement to which Gramsci was referring stemmed from a circular of 20 October 1920, issued by the commanding general's office to the army, that showed an ambiguous attitude (Alatri, 1961: 60) and from the fact that, between 1919 and 1921, half a million soldiers had been demobilised, which went from having around 880,000 to 330,000 active servicemen.

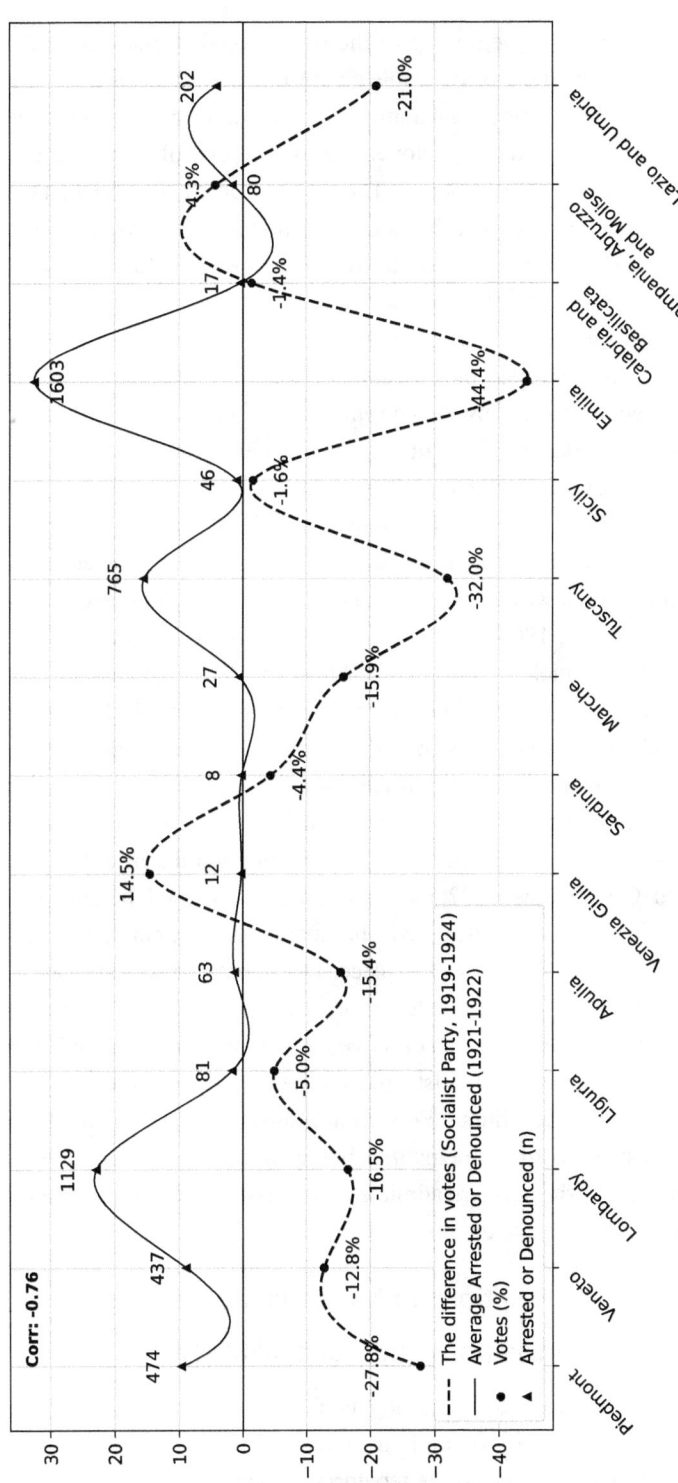

Figure 7 Fascist arrested or denounced/difference of vote for socialists (1919–24).

Symbolically, however, the beginning of the wave aimed at eradicating the socialist movement, understood as the whole galaxy of bodies such as the Work Cooperatives, the People's Houses, and administrations, was the storming of the Palazzo d'Accursio in Bologna on 21 November, which took place on the day of the inauguration of the new city council. The violence on that day created the overall impression, at the time, that the police did nothing to prevent clashes that had been foreseeable for days. The newly elected mayor, Enio Gnudi – a member of the maximalist fraction of the Socialist Party – never took office and, in his place, the prefect appointed a commissioner. New elections for the renewal of the council were held only two years later, in November 1922, in a climate already deeply marked by the entrenchment of the squadrists and the Mussolini government. Starting from that 21 November, and as the phenomenon of *squadrismo* grew, the Red Councils were hit, one by one, with surgical precision (Albanese, 2008: 31–42). The success of the fascist squadrists in Bologna also helped to build the myth of invincibility and led to a swelling of their ranks. Not only that, however, as it also contributed to the formation of a new type of fascism (De Felice, 1965: 617), relatively autonomous from that led by Mussolini from Milan, which would later be known as 'agrarian fascism'. In August 1922 the cycle of violence aimed at the dissolution of the Red Councils ended in Milan. Palazzo Marino, the seat of the municipal administration, had to be garrisoned by the army to prevent fascist attacks, in a context in which relations between the Socialist administration and Prefect Lusignoli, close to Giolitti and in favour of an agreement between the latter and the fascists, were extremely strained. On 3 August 1922, the fascists finally occupied the town hall and the prefect, in response, dismissed the mayor and appointed Count Ferdinando Lalli as Commissioner in his place. D'Annunzio also took part in the assault, boldly climbing onto the balcony of Palazzo Marino. At the end of August, the Ministry of the Interior also dissolved the Milanese city council. The 'success' in Milan intoxicated the fascists, paving the way for a further wave of violence against the Lombard Giunta. Following Franzinelli (2019: 118), 1921 witnessed the highest levels of municipalities being commissioned by prefects, with almost 80 per cent of the northern administration dissolved as a consequence of fascist attacks, resulting in the dismissal of mayors.

3 From the 1921 Elections to Mussolini as President

The 1921 Elections and National Blocs

On 6 April 1921, the decree dissolving the chamber was published. Formally, it was explained by the need to implement another decree, No. 1655 of 18 November 1920, which extended the territorial validity of the electoral law to the new provinces that had been ceded to the Kingdom of Italy by the Treaty of Rapallo, thus allowing them to vote. Behind this formal necessity, however, there was also a political purpose pursued by Giolitti, then prime minister. Having realised that socialism was experiencing a period of crisis, he tried to take advantage of the situation by calling elections for 15 May. Giolitti had already had Mussolini's far from foregone endorsement of the Rapallo peace accords, an endorsement that came in the wake of the future Duce's detachment from D'Annunzio and the experience of 'fiumanism', and aimed at definitively repositioning fascism as the party of the middle classes (Gentile, 2022: 7). In the dissolution decree, the need to re-establish social peace was mentioned as one of the causes for which the elections were called. This was somewhat paradoxical, if one thinks that Giolitti himself was going to stand as a candidate with the very people responsible for the violence that had shattered that social peace, forming a bloc of conservative formations in a similar manner to what had happened in France with Georges Clemenceau and along the lines of what had already been experienced in the administrative elections of 1920. However, the lists of this formation, taking the name 'National Blocs', did not run in all constituencies, and included nationalists, fascists, democrats, reformist socialists, and *Combattenti*. Candidates in the bloc included figures like Salandra, Bonomi, Giovanni Celesia (a former member of the Fascio parlamentare) and Roberto Farinacci. In Rome, for example, liberals, fascists, and nationalists stood as candidates together in the National Union, in which Luigi Federzoni, Alfredo Rocco, and Giuseppe Bottai presented themselves. In Brescia there was the 'constitutional bloc' with the Fascio littorio and the five-pointed star of the liberals as its symbol. Then there was the Fascio Democratico in Caserta and the Blocco Liberale Democratico in Turin, with Cesare Maria De Vecchi and Cesare Rossi for the fascists and Luigi Facta for the liberals.

The election campaign unfolded in a climate of profound violence, with fascists benefiting from the goodwill of prefects who tended to lean towards ministerial candidates. . On election day, there were twenty-nine dead, and the following day a further ten. The terrorist action of the fascist squads, fuelled by *Il Popolo d'Italia*, was aimed at completely eradicating socialist penetration (Gentile, 2022: 246), a dimension of violence which became a fundamental aspect in influencing the outcome of the competition. For the analysis of the results, again as in 1919, it was decided to standardise the constituencies with those of 1924 in order to obtain comparable data.

Electors increased significantly compared to the 1919 elections (Table 4), partly because the number of serving military personnel, who were not allowed to vote, had decreased drastically, from 880,041 to 343,956. Voters increased by one million out of a total of 11 million voters: from 5.7 million to 6.7, with

Table 4 Results of the 1921 Italian parliamentary elections.

Region	N. of Constituencies	N. of List	Average Voters	Electorate	Emigrants	Soldiers N.	(1919–21)	Voters N.	(1919–21)	Valid Votes
Piedmont	4	5	60.35%	1,169,055	34,547	30,773	−61%	676,166	−6%	666,143
Liguria	1	3	58.04%	423,169	9,013	16,716	−66%	288,818	−3%	230,682
Lombardy	4	4	71.64%	1,510,987	27,908	52,499	−63%	1,035,647	4%	1,024,839
Veneto	5	10	68.60%	1,002,524	22,871	40,020	−64%	655,865	11%	644,598
Venezia Giulia	5	6	60.53%	514,723	13,855	10,237		304,249		296,985
Emilia	2	2	66.78%	879,440	12,632	28,421	−73%	577,040	−4%	559,862
Tuscany	3	2	65.68%	915,397	21,330	32,109	−71%	574,471	3%	566,133
Marche	1	3	55.44%	359,995	27,008	12,065	−64%	180,279	5%	177,916
Lazio and Umbria	2	3	55.46%	648,591	15,861	21,600	−46%	343,042	1%	338,931
Abruzzo and Molise	2	8	56.71%	739,317	82,217	13,800	−49%	369,911	−1%	364,805
Campania	3	6	50.56%	849,572	33,103	20,930	−45%	407,659	−1%	402,199
Apulia	2	4	55.82%	674,956	13,922	15,244	−65%	364,360	0%	360,478
Calabria and Basilicata	2	4	55.34%	634,336	73,495	14,637	−42%	304,385	−1%	302,248
Sicily	3	13	47.98%	1,253,553	80,682	25,809	−61%	555,151	−2%	550,307
Sardinia	1	2	52.56%	245,553	4,227	9,096	−19%	122,887	−3%	122,065
Total	40	54	60%	11,821,168	472,671	343,956	−61%	6,759,930	1%	6,608,191

a participation rate of 59 per cent. Liguria, Lombardy, and Veneto were the regions where participation was highest, with rates around 70 per cent. Consistent with 1919, however, the southern regions voted in significantly smaller numbers, around 50 per cent. There were 330 re-elected members, a much higher figure than in 1919, when there had been 197.

Turning then to an analysis of the votes cast for each side (Table 5), the first observation to be made is that the Socialists and Communists, added together, lost an average of 3 per cent of the vote, falling from 32 per cent to 29 per cent in total, divided between 25 per cent of socialists and the remaining 4 per cent of communists. The decline, however, was not uniform in all constituencies. In Emilia, one of the regions where the action of the squadrismo had been heaviest, the drop was most consistent (−20 per cent), followed by Piedmont with −10 per cent and Marche with −8 per cent. The Socialists gained positions in the south, with growth in Campania of 6 per cent and in Calabria and Sardinia of 4 per cent, and managed to get deputies elected in all regions, with the exception of Venezia Giulia. The Socialists were thus overall, the most voted political force, close behind the Popular Party, who reached 20 per cent. The bloc lists obtained just under 20 per cent nation-ally and constituted themselves as the third force. This result is much more remarkable if one looks at the data broken down regionally: in Lazio and Umbria they obtained 46.67 per cent, in Sardinia 47 per cent, in Liguria, Lombardy, Emilia, and Tuscany an average of 30 per cent. The liberals outside the blocs obtained 81 percent in Abruzzo and Molise, and around 70 percent in Sicily, Campania, Calabria, and Basilicata. In many regions, for example Abruzzo, the Liberals (outside the bloc coalition) alone obtained 75 per cent. For Mussolini the elections were an undoubted personal success. In the Bologna constituency, as a candidate with the National Blocs, the leader of Fascism collected 73,000 preferences out of a total of 300,000 votes (about 24 per cent); in Milan, again with the bloc, 69,248 preferences out of a total of 49,8761 valid votes (13 per cent); a remarkable result if you think that, in 1919, in the same constituency, he had obtained 4,657 preferences. In many lists, the Fascist candidates were the ones who gathered the most preferences, showing a greater capacity to aggregate consensus than the Liberals. A tangible symbol of the fact that the fascists had a prominent role within the lists, and by no means a second-class one, was also the fact that in many regions, such as Lombardy and Emilia, the emblem of the blocs' list was that of the Fascio littorio. In Piedmont, the bloc stopped at 8 per cent. Giolitti, who had been a promoter of the blocs but had instead stood as a candidate in the 'Democratic Liberal Party', collected 30,825 preferences in his seat in Cuneo.

The experience of the blocs, born with the ambition to defeat socialism and to normalize Fascism, had proved to be a double-edged sword and had ended in defeat for the liberal world. Fascism still lacked a valid alliance and a foothold

Table 5 Results of the 1921 Italian parliamentary elections (parties).

Region	Socialists N.	%	Comunists N.	%	Socialists and Comunists (1919–21)	Popular Party N.	%	(1919–21)	Blocchi N.	%	Other Costituzionali N.	%	Others N.	%
Piedmont	190,759	28.6%	79,507	11.9%	−10.0%	146,905	22.1%	3.0%	53,367	8.0%	195,605	29.4%		
Liguria	54,368	23.6%	19,884	8.6%	0.7%	55,206	23.9%	3.6%	71,023	30.8%	11,318	4.9%	18,833	8.2%
Lombardy	430,017	42.0%	42,089	4.1%	0.0%	262,452	25.6%	−4.6%	261,317	25.5%	17,101	1.7%	11,863	1.2%
Veneto	187,281	29.1%	10,065	1.6%	−6.8%	230,835	35.8%	2.2%	83,814	12.3%	71,131	11.0%	61,472	9.5%
Venezia Giulia	64,261	21.6%	20,473	6.9%	28.5%	55,569	18.7%	18.7%	50,453	34.8%	39,411	13.3%	66,791	22.5%
Emilia	187,202	33.4%	29,284	5.2%	−20.1%	107,835	19.3%	0.4%	182,596	32.6%			52,946	9.5%
Tuscany	176,121	31.1%	59,579	10.5%	−2.2%	106,991	18.9%	−1.0%	183,239	32.4%	11,825	2.1%	28,428	5.0%
Marche	35,831	20.1%	9,415	5.3%	−8.2%	53,117	29.9%	2.5%	48,656	27.4%	14,802	8.3%	16,097	9.0%
Lazio and Umbria	84,555	24.9%	8,400	2.5%	−6.2%	66,804	19.7%	−2.7%	158,190	46.7%			20,982	6.2%
Abruzzo and Molise	33,091	9.1%	3,223	0.9%	−0.4%	32,318	8.9%	1.6%			296,178	81.2%		0.0%
Campania	44,306	11.0%	3,854	1.0%	6.0%	61,572	15.3%	−3.1%			279,565	69.5%	12,897	3.2%
Apulia	63,824	17.7%	9,274	2.6%	2.0%	36,428	10.1%	−0.4%	109,635	30.4%	127,733	35.4%	13,584	3.8%

Calabria and Basilicata	29,082	9.6%	3,361	1.1%	4.0%	44,859	14.8%	1.8%			224,075	74.1%	871	0.3%
Sicily	39,423	7.2%	6,311	1.1%	1.8%	72,485	13.2%	0.7%			418,575	76.1%	13,513	2.5%
Sardinia	15,310	12.5%		0.0%	3.9%	13,929	11.4%	−0.8%	57,718	47.3%	35,108	28.8%		0.0%
	1,631,435	**24.7%**	**304,719**	**4.6%**	**−3.0%**	**1,347,305**	**20.4%**	**−0.2%**	**1,260,007**	**19.1%**	**1,627,530**	**24.6%**	**318,277**	**4.8%**

in southern Italy: here, however, Mussolini's forces, regardless of the poor result in terms of deputies (only thirty-six)[24] gained great prestige in this round. Immediately after the elections, as was to be expected, the blocs fell apart and eleven groups were formed in the lower house. This meant that a fragmented parliament had emerged from the elections, with the Liberals further weakened. Suffice it to say, for example, that the parliamentary commissions – which played a fundamental role in linking the chamber to the government – were composed of twenty-six members, divided as follows: six Socialists, one Communist, one Social Reformist, five Popular, ten from the liberal area, two Fascists and one Nationalist.

As shown in the Figure 8 and Table 6 summarising the election results, the Fascists managed to get 36 deputies elected (the largest groups originated from Emilia, with 7, followed by Lombardy with 5, and both Tuscany and Veneto with 4 each). The Constitutional forces had the support of a total of 200 deputies, constituting approximately 40 per cent of the Chamber of Deputies (or 242 adding the Nationalists), the Socialists had 124, the Popular Party 108 and the Communists 15. The total number of deputies belonging to the mass parties (Socialists, Communists, Populars, and Fascists) was substantial; together, they thus constituted by far the majority (283 out of 535). Furthermore, the Popular Party would be decisive for any majority, while, for the first time, the contribution of the Fascists could also become central..

In 1921, the number of deputies belonging to mass integration parties in the lower house increased after the 1919 elections (Table 6). Of the chamber, 52.9 per cent was composed of members from the Popular, Socialist, Communist, or Fascist parties, marking a 2.5 per cent increase from 1919. The most significant growth occurred in Liguria, Abruzzi, and Sicily. The average representation of mass parties in the central regions was 58 per cent (Figure 8). In the north, they accounted for more than 70 per cent. The south continued to be the stronghold of constitutional forces, with more than 60 per cent of the deputies and the area where the number of Fascist deputies was the lowest (less than 1%).

The right-wing formations and, more broadly, the liberal world, it must be remembered, did not coincide: the right was not necessarily the liberal world, just as not all the liberal world was right wing. After the double defeats of 1919 and 1921, however, the right had not yet emerged from the liberal logic of loosely structured formations, and the liberal left was essentially significantly diminished to the point of near invisibility. After years of debate and failed

---

[24] Normally the figure of thirty-five deputies is reported, proposed by the *Corriere della Sera* on 21 June 1921. In the 'Statistica delle elezioni generali politiche per la XXVI Legislatura', presented in December 1923 and published in 1924, the figure is thirty-six. Ministero dell'economia nazionale, Direzione Generale della Statistica (1924a).

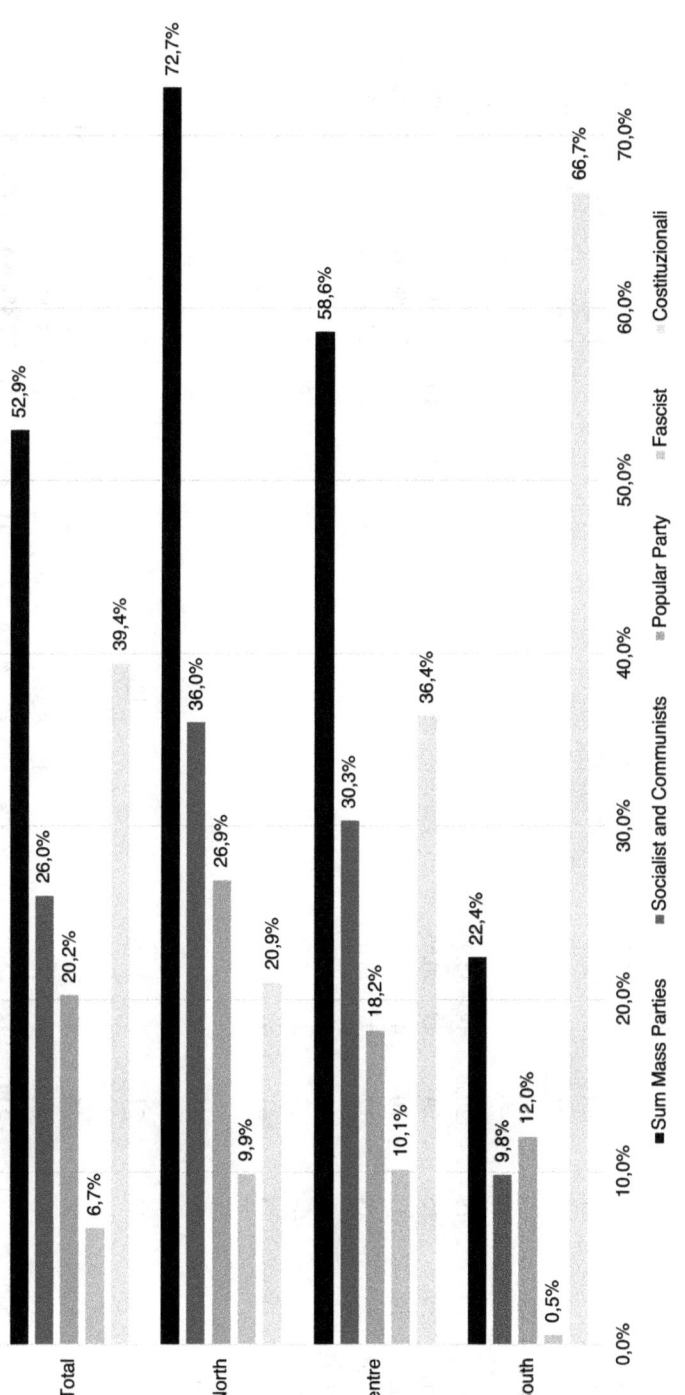

Figure 8 Percentage of deputies (mass integration parties/constitutionals), 1921.

Table 6 Percentage of deputies (mass integration parties/Constitutionals), 1921.

Region	N. of deputies	Newly elected MPs	Re-elected MPs	Socialist N.	%	Communist N.	%	Popular N.	%	Fascist N.	%	Nationalist N.	%	Costituzionali N.	%	Other N.	%	Mass Integration Parties %	Mass Integration (1919–1921)
Piedmont	56	17	38	16	28.6%	5	8.9%	12	21.4%	3	5.4%	1	1.8%	19	33.9%			64.3%	−7.1%
Liguria	17	4	13	4	23.5%	1	5.9%	5	29.4%	2	11.8%	1	5.9%	3	17.6%	1	5.9%	70.6%	11.8%
Lombardy	64	18	44	27	42.2%	1	1.6%	19	29.7%	5	7.8%			11	17.2%	1	1.6%	81.3%	1.6%
Veneto	50	17	31	17	34.0%			19	38.0%	4	8.0%			7	14.0%	2	4.0%	80.0%	3.9%
New provinces	27			2	7.4%	2	7.4%	5	18.5%	4	14.8%	1	3.7%	3	11.1%	10	37.0%	48.1%	
Emilia	39	19	20	14	35.9%	2	5.1%	8	20.5%	7	17.9%			7	17.9%	2	5.1%	79.5%	−4.2%
Tuscany	39	15	24	12	30.8%	3	7.7%	8	20.5%	4	10.3%			10	25.6%	2	5.1%	69.2%	2.6%
Marche	17	7	10	4	23.5%	1	5.9%	5	29.4%	1	5.9%			5	29.4%	1	5.9%	64.7%	5.9%
Lazio and Umbria	25	13	12	7	28.0%			4	16.0%	3	12.0%	3	12.0%	7	28.0%	1	4.0%	56.0%	0.0%
Abruzzo	18	6	12	3	16.7%			1	5.6%	2	11.1%	1	5.6%	10	55.6%	1	5.6%	33.3%	19.5%
Campania and Molise	58	15	41	4	6.9%			9	15.5%			2	3.4%	38	65.5%	6	10.3%	22.4%	−3.1%
Apulia	28	8	20	6	21.4%			2	7.1%	1	3.6%			19	67.9%			32.1%	7.1%
Calabria and Basilicata	33	12	21	3	9.1%			3	9.1%			1	3.0%	19	57.6%	6	18.2%	18.2%	6.1%
Sicily	52	16	36	4	7.7%			7	13.5%			1	1.9%	32	61.5%	8	15.4%	21.2%	9.6%
Sardinia	12	4	8	1	8.3%			1	8.3%					10	83.3%			16.7%	8.3%
Total	535	171	330	124	23.2%	15	2.8%	108	20.2%	36	6.7%	11	2.1%	200	37.4%	41	7.7%	52.9%	2.5%

attempts to counter the decline and regain positions after the defeat of 1919, a few days after the March on Rome, in October 1922, the Liberal Party was finally born. Even in its infancy, however, the Liberal Party was, in fact, already on its last legs. The great representatives of the liberal world, including Giolitti and Salandra, initially looked at this experiment with diffidence, so much so that they did not participate in the founding convention held in Bologna that year. Then, they later joined it. With them were other leading figures of liberalism, such as Sidney Sonnino, Orlando, Benedetto Croce, and Gaetano Mosca.

From Revolutionary Fascism to Integration into the Blocs

The Fasci di Combattimento movement was also a very confused amalgam and, at least until November 1920, a marginal one. The fascist movement had been a secondary phenomenon which had started to swell from November 1920 to become a mass phenomenon from the summer of 1921. After the electoral defeat of 1919 and the results of 1921, however, a profound and, again, erratic and undulating transformation process began. Indeed, under the generic term *fascism* hid a multitude of different phenomena that evolved seamlessly and in a very contradictory manner over the years. Mussolinism and an important part of squadrism, for example, did not always coincide either in intent or place. In fact, *squadrismo* often developed independently of Mussolini's orientations, in areas that were not easily controlled by him, such as Emilia, Veneto, and Tuscany; that is, the areas with the highest socialist settlement, and almost exclusively in an anti-socialist function.

Mussolini himself, moreover, had often changed positions: first an exponent of the maximalist wing of the Socialist Party, then, in 1915, founder of the newspaper *Il Popolo d'Italia*, as is well known, he had switched from neutralism to interventionism, being expelled from the Socialist Party for this. On 23 March 1919, Mussolini and a small number of militants had gathered in the hall of the Circolo dell'Alleanza Industriale in Milan to found the Fasci Italiani di Combattimento movement. The so-called San Sepolcro Programme, on which the movement's activities were to be based, was published in *Il Popolo d'Italia* on 6 June of the same year. With regard to the definition of the relationship between the state and the citizens, the programme was undoubtedly hyper-democratic. At the first point it proposed 'universal suffrage by regional list voting with proportional representation, voting and eligibility for women', 'the abolition of the Senate' and the 'convocation of a National Assembly whose first task would be to establish the form of constitution of the State'.[25] A second u-turn by Mussolini distanced him, towards the end of 1920, from

---

[25] 'Per il problema politico', *Il Popolo d'Italia*, 6 June (1919).

these initial positions of the movement he had founded (De Felice, 1965: 3). Finally, marking the need for a turning point came the parliamentarisation of the movement. The 'revolutionary' charge of the *fascismo della prima ora* had already been substantially exhausted when Giolitti called the fascists to his lists along with nationalists and liberals. The National Blocs, which were aimed at seeking a stabilising majority in the Italian political system, turned instead into the exact opposite. On 30 June 1921, Mussolini, together with Bottai, went to the king for the first consultations for the formation of the new government.[26] This aspect is particularly significant considering, for example, that the Socialists had consistently refused to participate in the consultations. The meetings at the Quirinale were not merely ceremonial; they substantively determined which political forces were granted access to a privileged, 'governable' circuit. On 24 July, Mussolini announced to the Chamber of Deputies that Fascism would withhold its vote of confidence from the Bonomi government for 'sentimental rather than political reasons' but that, in the future, he would reserve the option to vote in favour. The most surprising statement in that speech, however, lies in the wishes Mussolini formulated for a government composed entirely of the three mass parties, Popular, Socialist, and Fascist.[27] It was a possible hypothesis on paper, given that the three formations had a majority, albeit a very small one (268 out of 535 deputies). It was a fleeting vision, but ultimately leading to no tangible outcomes. On 3 August 1921; that is, a few weeks after the political elections of 15 May, the pacification pact between the socialists and fascists was concluded. The peace pact could have led to a kind of Labour government (De Bernardi, 2022: 73), but it did not come to pass because the squadrist wing of the fascist movement turned against Mussolini, who was then far from being an undisputed leader. Thus opened the first serious internal crisis within fascism: a real turning point. A bitter dispute took shape between the squadrist wing and the political wing of the party, which went so far as to challenge the primacy of Fascism. Following Emilio Gentile's view, the fact that a reconciliation between the rebels and Mussolini was quickly reached should not have led to belittling the episode, in which Mussolini himself was accused of treason or separatism (Gentile, 2022: 361–2). Mussolini's vision, which had led to the pacification pact, disregarded the deeper moods of a movement that had been forged precisely against socialism. In fact, it was no coincidence that a large part of the fascist militants was against the pact, especially the more extreme fringes linked to squadrism such

---

[26] *Corriere della Sera*, 1 July (1921).

[27] B. Mussolini, 'Speech delivered to the Chamber of Deputies on 23 July 1921', in Regno d'Italia, Camera dei Deputati, *Atti Parlamentari, Legislatura XXVI, Tornata del 23 luglio 1921*, https://storia.camera.it/regno/lavori/leg26/sed016.pdf.

as Dino Grandi and Piero Marsich. The squadrist actions followed one another in those days as if the pact had not even been signed and the regional congress of the Fasci Emiliani refused to support Mussolini who, therefore, announced his resignation on 18 August. Within a few weeks, the pacification pact was buried. Mussolini and the party realised they could not live without each other and the opening to the socialists was definitively cancelled in the name of realism (De Felice, 1966: 139–71).

From the end of August, fascism veered to the right once and for all, occupying a space already occupied by nationalists and conservative liberals. Once the groups were formed in the low chamber, the liberals (Salandra's conservative wing), nationalists and fascists began to deepen relations and hold meetings, forming a more or less formal group that consulted on the formation of new governments.[28] The group that came to be known in the media as the 'Right' was born.[29] In November, the fascist movement became a party, Partito Nazionale Fascista (National Fascist Party – PNF) and gave itself a statute. After the events of the summer, Mussolini needed to give the new formation a deeply hierarchical and centralised structure based on the idea of the party-militia. The year 1921 was thus a complete turnaround from 1919, and the statute of the newly formed PNF traced some of the lines of the conservative right, that had always seen the organism of the state and the minimal state as the main programmatic pillars: thus it was declared that the Fascist Party's vision was of a 'state that must be reduced to its essential functions of a political and juridical order' and of the 'necessity of arriving principally at the reorganisation of state budgets [...] the strict protection of taxpayers' money, the restitution to private industry of the industrial enterprises to the management of which the state has proved unsuitable'.[30]

The alliance between Nationalists and Fascists came in 1923. In the course of time, especially with the various twists and turns of fascism, the ties between them had become stronger and stronger, but each of the contenders was still fighting its own battle. The relations between nationalists and fascists were, therefore, very complex and marked by mistrust: the Nationalists did not like the more 'socialist' side of fascism, and the Fascists did not like the excessive class-conservatism of the nationalists.

The Socialist Split

In this context, the Liberals maintained government leadership, initially with Bonomi (July 1921–February 1922), a social reformist, and subsequently with Luigi Facta, both of whom were elected as part of the blocs. The umpteenth

---

[28] *Corriere della Sera*, 1 July (1921). [29] *Corriere della Sera*, 5 February (1922).
[30] *Corriere della Sera*, 28 December (1921).

crisis involving the first Facta government (February–August 1922) forced the parties to reposition themselves or at least seek alternative solutions. From the spring of 1922, Popular Party and Socialist collaborators sought a dialogue to open an understanding, but the attempt proved to be an uphill struggle.[31] On 18 July, the *Corriere della Sera* reported movements within the Popular and the Socialist Parties. Turati, Giuseppe Emanuele Modigliani, Elia Musatti, and Giacomo Matteotti tried to open a collaborative discussion that could lead to an alliance between the Popular, Democrats, and Socialists. Nevertheless, the Democrats (left wings of the constitutionals forces) and Popular Party remained reluctant to collaborate with the Socialists. On 29 July 1922, Turati, the leader of the reformist faction within the Socialist Party, accepted King Vittorio Emanuele III's invitation to participate in consultations for the formation of a new government. Turati's decision to accept represented an act of defiance against the directives of the Socialist leadership. The *Corriere della Sera* speculated on various hypotheses, including the possibility of forming a government that included the Fascists, an option that Turati rejected.[32] A hypothetical government led by Orlando, purportedly comprising both Socialist and Fascist members, fell through, leading to Facta being appointed to form a new government.

Over time, the Italian political situation steadily worsened. The pacification pact of August 1921 had served no purpose and the whole socialist world of cooperatives, People's Houses and communes was dissolving. The elections of 1921 had certainly marked a defeat. Yet, despite everything, the Socialists had remained united. A year later, everything had changed. On 4 October 1922, the Partito Socialista Unitario (United Socialist Party) was founded with Matteotti as its secretary with the reformist component being expelled from the party: certain positions had become irreconcilable. The vast majority of the parliamentary group remained with Turati. The principal bone of contention was the attitude to be taken towards the government. Turati's gradualists sought an agreement, while Serrati opposed it. The Serrati motion ultimately prevailed, albeit by a narrow margin (Spriano, 1967: 223–4).

From the Facta Government to the Mussolini Government

The second Facta government (August–October 1922) had a difficult life and finding a stable majority, given the mistrust between all formations, had become effectively impossible. Mussolini had already been in negotiations for some time with Giolitti, Facta, and Salandra (Gentile, 2014) to become part of

---

[31] 'Tra socialisti e popolari – Primizie collaborazionistiche', *Corriere della Sera*, 12 March (1922).
[32] *Corriere della Sera*, 30 July (1922).

a government. He was therefore, at that point, anything but an alien in the area of government. The rightly preponderant emphasis given to the March on Rome and its preparation by most historiography, however, means that all the surrounding events, occurring before, during, and after, are relegated to a secondary position. Much has been written about the March on Rome and we do not want to go into it here (see, among others, Albanese, 2008). What is important to underline here are two aspects: the crisis of the Facta government and the negotiation process for the new government. We will focus, therefore, only on those aspects that directly impacted the sequence that led to Mussolini's appointment, by trying to restore the complexity of the days between 27 and 31 October 1922.

After the Fascist convention in Naples on 4 October 1922, the centre of gravity of events, which inevitably also had repercussions on the formation of the government, centred on three cities: Perugia, where the command of the march was located; Rome the capital and the king's seat at the Quirinale; and Milan, the city where Mussolini lived. On 26 October, the ministers of the Facta government put their portfolios back to the prime minister, bringing an end to the cabinet. The involvement of the Fascists in the government that was to be formed was a fact that was already taken for granted, so much so that the names of the ministers and the relative ministries to be assigned to them were also given.[33] In order to understand the atmosphere of the period, it is also necessary to emphasise how the daily *Il Giornale d'Italia* had become a sort of bridge between the right and Fascism and, which more than any other, promoted the idea of a government to be led either by Mussolini or Salandra.[34] Orlando was already in Piedmont that day to speak with Giolitti. Mussolini was in Milan. The crisis at the end of October 1922 witnessed the overlapping of two distinct yet intertwined but also separated issues: the March on Rome on one hand, and the government crisis on the other. In the afternoon of Friday, October 27, the king returned to Rome and met Facta at the train station, where Facta announced his resignation. Early on October 28, Prefect Lusignoli informed the Ministry of the Interior that an insurrection was underway. Following this, the Council of Ministers convened and unanimously approved a declaration of a state of siege to protect Rome from the squads; however, the king did not countersign the decree, nullifying its validity. On the same day, Luigi Federzoni and Giacomo Acerbo attempted to persuade Mussolini to accept the leadership of a new government, potentially under Salandra or Orlando. In the early afternoon, according to the reconstructions provided by the Corriere della Sera, to

---

[33] *Corriere della Sera*, 28 October (1922).
[34] Essentially, the *Giornale d'Italia* considered the Chamber elected in 1921 to be delegitimised by events, advocated for electoral reform, viewed the Popolari as delegitimised by the Holy See, and regarded fascism as the true emerging force of the time. See *Giornale d'Italia*, October 1922.

which we have added those of Emilio Gentile (2014: 312–15), the king began a series of consultations to form a new government, starting with Enrico De Nicola, the president of the Chamber of Deputies, and including a meeting with Salandra. During this process, the prefect of Milan contacted Prime Minister Facta to relay Mussolini's aspiration to be appointed as prime minister. By the end of the day, the king's first choice was Salandra but, on the following day, October 29, Salandra declined the invitation. *Corriere della Sera*[35] reported that some unidentified Lombard deputies had telegraphed Salandra, suggesting that Mussolini would be a preferable choice and noting that 'the Confederations of Industry and Agriculture were leaning in the same direction'. On the morning of October 29, Grandi called Mussolini to inform him that he had been appointed prime minister. Mussolini then took the train from Milan to Rome on 29 October and arrived the next day to be appointed as Presidente del Consiglio (Prime Minister). Only after concluding the negotiation process to form a new government, on Tuesday 31 October, were the squadrists allowed to enter Rome. They paraded from Piazza del Popolo through the Quirinale – where the king welcomed and greeted them – in a procession that lasted more than five hours, eventually reaching the Altare della Patria to pay homage to the unknown soldier. The three days between 27 and 31 October, the change from Facta's government to Mussolini's was thus made. However, other proposals had also circulated in between, with at least two of these coming from Orlando and Salandra; the figures closest to Mussolini. It was not the failure to countersign the state of siege, therefore, that had opened the capital to the squadrists. On the contrary, the king's failure to sign the decree, anything but solitary and sudden, could be placed within a complex negotiating process full of twists and turns. Mussolini's entourage – Acerbo, Galeazzo Ciano, Federzoni, Grandi, De Vecchi – had at first appeared open to a solution that did not see Mussolini as prime minister. But, with Salandra's resignation, Mussolini became the new head of government. A new phase was beginning in which a certain consensus was forming around Mussolini and the government he was proposing, especially among liberals and the conservative Popular Party.

We are thus faced with a new stage in a process of the *critical junctures* that would last more than two years, until Mussolini, with his speech in January 1925, set the stage for the formalisation of the dictatorship. The historical period that had opened up powerfully with the end of the First World War and the elections of 1919 had seen the political strategies that had characterised the pre-war period fade away. Giolitti and Salandra, along with the other liberal leaders, had failed to interpret the changes that the era had brought, above all, the irruption of the

---

[35] *Corriere della Sera*, 31 October 1922.

masses as the main protagonists of the new period. Since the demonstrations of the 'radiant May' of 1915, it had already become clear that politics had changed and that the masses played a fundamental role in the processes of legitimisation, both on the left and on the right. The March on Rome, in this sense, must also be seen as marking a long trajectory that began in 1915. There was, undoubtedly, a lack of understanding of what was happening rather than ambiguity: an incomprehension that led part of the liberal class to fail to realise that, behind the squadrists, there was a real political movement (Gentile, 2014: 345). Mussolini, on the other hand, had manoeuvred cynically and very casually on several fronts, but, above all, he had understood that it was the conservatives who needed a leader. In siding with the right, he brought to the right what he did not have: the rising, nationalist, middle-class masses. He won over Salandra precisely because, in the negotiation process with the king for the new government, he proved himself far better able than his opponent to interpret the political climate and the country.

The First Steps of Mussolini's Coalition Government

On 17 November 1922, the Mussolini government won a vote of confidence in the Chamber of Deputies. There were 429 members present, of these, 7 abstained, 306 were in favour, and 116 were against. Voting in favour were the Fascists, Nationalists, the *Costituzionali* (right-wing Liberals and Democrats), and the Popular Party. Voting against them were the Unitary Socialists, Maximalists, Communists, Republicans, and the two deputies of the Sardinian Action Party (Umberto Cao and Emilio Lussu).[36] The first phase of Mussolini's rule (November 1922–January 1925) was meant to be the final attempt made by the head of state and liberal groups to stop the political system from capitulating to mass party rules, notably those of the Socialists. The power of the head of state (De Felice, 1966: 120–5) during this critical juncture was far from merely symbolic; it had a big impact on the balance of the entire political system. The stance taken by King Vittorio Emanuele III was somehow paradoxical. He favoured disloyal forces, the Fascists, to avoid other perceived disloyal forces, namely the Socialists with the support of some loyal forces, accessing power. The Crown supported Mussolini at every step, leading to the foundation of the authoritarian regime and through all the crises in his first two years in office (De Bernardi, 2022: 81).

The first Mussolini government was made up of a coalition of the PNF, various liberal formations, members of the Popular Party and the Nationalists. The PNF was clearly the dominant force in the government, not only because of

---

[36] *Corriere della Sera*, 18 November (1922).

its nine ministries (about 41 per cent of the entire government), but also due to the relevance of those ministries. In addition to the premiership, Fascists headed the ministries of the Interior, Foreign Affairs, Finance, and Justice. That is, ministerial careers were characterised by belonging to the inner circle of the foundational group of the PNF. Liberals obtained only six ministries, 27.3 per cent; the Popular Party, 13.6 per cent; and the Nationalists (the closest ally of the PNF until 1923 when it joined the PNF), 18.2 per cent. Of the ministries, 10 per cent were led by outsiders and 10% by figures from the armed forces (Adinolfi, 2022). The emergence of new parties in the government – the PNF and the Nationalists – was not the only signal of a substantial rupture with the previous tradition. However, this rupture resulted in the inclusion of a new class of politicians-parliamentarians; 46.4 per cent of the ministers had been elected in the parliamentarian elections of 1921–4 and only 17.9 per cent before the First World War. More than 20 per cent of ministers had no parliamentary background, and almost 68 per cent had very little political experience (between one and five years in parliament).

Local Elections for Dissolved Municipalities

From September 1922, in the phase immediately preceding Mussolini's rise to the prime ministership, a new cycle of elections for the renewal of municipal councils began. As we saw immediately after the administrative elections of 1920, which had led to many cities being governed by the Socialists, Fascist violence erupted. The purpose was to provoke the dissolution of the city councils and to induce the prefects to appoint commissioners who would replace the elected mayors. Within a short time, the squadrism and the prefects had succeeded in having most administrations dissolved, mainly in the north and predominantly socialist, but not only those. Turin, for example, was also commissioned following a crisis that had been provoked by the fascists and whose clear aim was to replace the liberal mayor Riccardo Cattaneo. At a time when it was on the eve of legislative elections, the government wanted to avoid having a figure at the head of the municipality who would show signs of independence. In Rome, another city where the Socialists were in opposition, it was instead the Nationalists who triggered the crisis in the municipal council.

If the administrative cycle of 1920 had been long but characterised by a minimum of organicity, this time the round extended throughout 1922 and 1923. The votes immediately took on the character of a general test of the tightness of the new party and constitutional structure of which the PNF had become the pivot, with the Popular Party and Liberals as government allies, but

Rise of Mass Parties, Liberal Italy, and Fascist Dawn (1919–1924)

in a subordinate function; a very different scenario from the one in which the 1921 elections had been held.

The round of elections began shortly before the March on Rome and allows us to grasp what the climate of the time was immediately before Mussolini became prime minister. Suffice it to cite one case among all: Milan. On 18 October 1922, the Milan branch of the Popular Party decided to hold a referendum among its members to determine whether or not to ally with the Fascists. Giovan Battista Migliori in the assembly was in favour of an alliance with the Fascists, but the issue was by no means unanimous within the party.[37] In the meantime, however, the same bloc as in 1920 had been reconstituted, which, along with the representatives of the Fascio Milanese, was also joined by the shopkeepers' associations and the Industrial Federation. Right from the start, the rhetoric of the non-partisan nature of the elections, which were supposed to have, it was said, a restorative character, came forward. That is, after what was described as the 'devastation' of the municipal coffers caused by the squandering of the socialist administrations,[38] the elections were supposed to restore the municipality's finances and balance its budget. The Milanese bloc, as obvious and predictable, won with 87,368 votes and 57.4 per cent of the vote, thus winning 64 seats on the municipal council.[39] To the Maximalist Socialists went just 17,000 votes, corresponding to only one seat. Instead, almost 50,000 votes were given to the Unitarian Socialists, who won 15 seats. Thus ended the last election with some pluralist content of the entire administrative election cycle and definitively ended what had been more of a revenge than a political battle, brooded over by the entire middle class against the socialist administrations of Emilio Caldara in 1914 and Angelo Filippetti (1920–2).[40] Milan, the country's economic capital, became the focal point of an election. In 1920, the Socialists had won by a narrow margin, highlighting the divide between socialist and constitutional forces. By 1922, however, this gap had shifted, with the Milanese bloc gaining a majority and the Unitarian Socialists securing only a smaller representation on the council.

Following Milan, a series of further conquests ensued. In Bologna, in January 1923, three years after the massacre at the Palazzo d'Accursio, the administration was still managed by a prefectural commissioner after the previous dissolution. Elections were held without the Socialists even having the chance to present their own list. The Bolognese elections were directly managed by Leandro Arpinati, a Fascist deputy and squadrist, who made it an exclusively Fascist affair. The winner was obviously the 'National Blocs' list and Umberto

---

[37] *Corriere della Sera*, 18 October (1922). [38] *Corriere della Sera*, 28 October (1922).
[39] *Corriere della Sera*, 11 December (1922). [40] *Corriere della Sera*, 12 December (1922).

Puppini, also a Fascist, was elected mayor with 41,000 votes out of 62,000 registered voters.[41] In Reggio Emilia, two lists stood as candidates, that of the Fascist Party and that of the Popular Party. The Fascists won, after twenty-five years of uninterrupted Socialist government.[42] In December, it was the turn of the Mantuan municipalities, where the Fascists presented themselves with two lists: both the majority and the minority lists. The same dynamics occurred in the municipalities in the province of Modena, while in the province of Bergamo, the last Socialist municipalities were dissolved. Another modality was that of the single list aggregating all parties, within which the Fascist naturally prevailed, as in the case of Ferrara. Or as in Alessandria, where socialists had governed since 1914, in Terni, Spoleto, and Gubbio, all Socialist administrations. There were few places where the Fascists did not obtain a majority in generally very small municipalities, such as Monza. A singular element to note is the fact that the *Corriere della Sera*, faced with such a situation, described these elections with great emphasis on their democratic nature and participation.[43]

The Italian political system had never accepted the Socialists, but was forced to deal with them. These local elections, taking place after a long cycle of commissariats, therefore represented a vengeance that had been meticulously carried out against all the shrines of the red administrations and whose instigators, the Fascists, could not be considered exclusively. This is clear from the pages of the *Corriere della Sera*, which in those days took up the themes of a 1920 editorial in which it spoke of the violence of the fascist squads against the socialists. The point that clearly emerged was that the Socialists were considered the real culprits for having created an environment of political hatred; a climate that had led to a widespread feeling of hostility in public opinion, which was then exploited by fascism. The aim of the liberals and conservatives, therefore, was a return to legality outside of revolutionary paradigms and, to achieve this end, paradoxically, they considered the Fascists to be the most suitable. The local elections of 1922–3 therefore had multiple functions, first and foremost that of definitively eliminating the forces considered by liberals and conservatives to be anti-national, that is, the Socialists: on this level there was almost unanimous agreement between liberals, populars, and fascists. They were then used by the fascists to delegitimise the Chamber of Deputies and, in particular, its socialist component. The syllogism is quite simple: if the Socialists had lost all the cities, it was because they no longer had the consensus they had had in 1919 or 1920.

---

[41] *Corriere della Sera*, 23 January (1923).

[42] 'The administrative elections in Reggio Emilia were held with complete freedom. 70% voted and in some sections, 90%. Thus, after 25 years of almost uninterrupted government, the Reggio Emilia socialist administration fell', *Corriere della Sera*, 14 November (1922).

[43] *Corriere della Sera*, 18 December (1922).

4 The 1924 Elections

The New Electoral Law

On 6 June 1923, the Council of Ministers unanimously approved the electoral reform proposal put forward by Acerbo, the fascist Undersecretary of State to the Prime Minister's Office. The new draft established a single national constituency. Under this system, any list receiving more than 25 per cent of the votes would be entitled to two-thirds of the 535 parliamentary seats. The remaining third of the parliamentary seats would be elected proportionally in regional constituencies. Consequently, it was a law that endowed party leadership with significant powers, lacking any countervailing measures to curb the prerogatives of a government-backed by a large parliamentary majority. The logic was precisely the opposite compared to the previous and hitherto existing law, which guaranteed strong local autonomies.

The necessary majority in parliament to approve the reform was not assured. On the one hand, the Liberals were mostly in favour; on the other, the Socialist factions (Unitarians and Maximalists), along with the Communists, opposed it. Caught in the middle were the Popolari, who were part of the cabinet; still supported Mussolini's government; but were undecided about whether to approve the bill. Alcide De Gasperi, one of the major leaders of the Popular Party, expressed his dissent on the law even before the draft was taken to the Council of Ministers. The majority of the Popular Party – and with them, some Liberals and Democrats – were not openly opposed but merely indicated that they would have preferred the majority prize to be triggered above 40 per cent and reduced from two-thirds to three-fifths; that is, a reduction of 35 seats. In this way, they intended to prevent the government from being tempted to use parallel lists to grab deputies in the remaining third. In the pages of his *Corriere d'Italia*, the opinions of the internal conservative Catholic faction were collected, vehemently in favour of supporting the government in every respect, once again openly contrasting with the official party line.

In June, the parliamentary commission known as the 'Committee of 18', was appointed to scrutinise the law. It included the most important political leaders in a balance that did not reflect the proportion of the forces represented in the chamber. The Socialists and Communists had three representatives despite having 30 per cent of the deputies; the Fascists substantially three (despite having less than 10 per cent of the deputies); the Popular Party had two (20 per cent); the Liberals had nine (about 50 per cent) and the Social Reformists one. The commission's president was Giolitti, a decisive figure in the law's approval. The commission raised two critical points regarding the new law. On the one hand, the relationship between the government and the parliament, the new law promoted an executive majority that nullified any power of control of the lower house. On the other, the relationship between parties and the individual MPs, because with proportional representation and the single national constituency, all power of individuals was cancelled in favour of party hierarchies.

For Mussolini, the non-negotiable elements of the reform were the single college system, majority bonus, and regional proportional representation. In the liberal world, it quickly became evident that the approval of the new law would lead to a bargaining process: support for the law in exchange for inclusion on the electoral list envisioned by Mussolini. Many deputies, especially in the south where fascism was still weak, aimed to secure a place on what was expected to be the winning list. Thus, the calculations of many Liberals were largely opportunistic. Giolitti and Salandra, for example, were not against it but would have preferred to return to the single-member constituency. This system would have allowed them to maintain the clientele system of the liberal period. Giolitti himself and Luigi Fera, the former from Piedmont and the latter from the south, were not against the law per se but they were against the national distribution of seats for the majority parties. That is, they believed that this proportion should have been related to the margin that the winning list had in each constituency and that, therefore, for example, in Piedmont and the south, the lists that did not run with that government should have been entitled to a greater number of deputies. At the opposite end of the spectrum were the Liberal leaders from areas where fascism was strongest, who saw the strict principle of the law as a way of salvation. Former prime minister Orlando shared the idea of the subordination of minorities that the new law would have introduced to the need to create a stable governing majority that would guarantee a return to normal constitutional life.

The impression that the electoral law would upset the constitutional order was beginning to be widespread, and the feeling that a totalitarian state was in the making was timidly beginning to emerge. Bonomi sensed that such a law would have introduced an identification of the party with the state so profound that it would no longer allow any distinction between the two institutions. Giovanni Amendola, who among the Liberals, would later most strongly oppose fascism, began to refer to the situation created by calling it totalitarian.[44] Even the *Corriere della Sera* suggested that the electoral law – which few wanted but which many supported, hoping for a normalisation of fascism – could have led to an authoritarian involution of the system.[45]

As for the procedure to be followed, three positions emerged within the commission: one opposed proceeding to the discussion of the articles in

---

[44] Giovanni Amendola, *Il Mondo*, 12 May 1923.   [45] *Corriere della Sera*, 27 June (1923).

parliament; another objected partly to the law's guiding principles and called for revisions; and a third was in favour. Despite these divisions, the law ultimately passed, overcoming initial opposition, with Giolitti voting in favour of proceeding to discuss the articles. Of the eighteen members of the committee, eight voted against.[46] Thus, the work of the commission ended on 4 July and the parliamentary debate began on 9 July. The outcome of the parliamentary process of the law continued to be anything but certain for some time, the uncertainty of which Mussolini was well aware of and who intended, from the outset, to strike at those who, due to their position, could have represented a danger. At that time, there were three main enemies: Don Sturzo, Turati, and Luigi Albertini, director of *Corriere della Sera*. The political climate around fascism thus changed considerably, generating a malaise that led some segments of the liberal and popular world, who had been in favour of it at first, to begin to distance themselves from it. However, the preponderant part of the liberal world, which had by then moved closer to fascism, embraced the climate of open confrontation, aligning itself with Mussolini's rhetoric as he attended all the debates in the chamber. The pressure on the parties became very strong. The dissent that pitted the clerical moderates against the more dubious wing of fascism grew until Sturzo was forced to resign (De Rosa, 1972: 223–54). However, this did not lead to substantial changes in the party line. Amendola highlighted that the significant parliamentary support for fascism was not actually driven by a desire to consolidate power in a single party but, rather, by the need to restore public order.[47]

Shortly afterwards, on 15 July, the chamber was called upon to give confidence to the government, which was resolved with 303 votes in favour and 140 against, and to approve the passage of the discussion of the individual articles of the Acerbo Law. This motion finally passed with 235 votes in favour (thus far from the absolute majority of 268 votes), 139 against, and 77 abstentions. The progress of the approval process for the new electoral law was saved by a direct intervention by Mussolini, who had managed to change the Popular Party's positions at the last moment. At a meeting of the leadership of the Catholic parliamentarians, a motion had passed that shifted the popular vote from a vote against to an abstention. The change was approved by 41 of their deputies, while 39 remained against it. In the chamber, 9 moderate Catholics voted in favour and were expelled from the party. Bonomi and Amendola, although hesitant, abstained. On 21 July, the chamber thus gave its final assent by secret ballot. Two hundred deputies were absent, and the votes in favour were

---

[46] De Gasperi and Micheli (Popular), Bonomi (Socialist), Alfredo Falcioni (Constitutional), Turati (Unionist), Antonio Graziadei (Communist), Eugenio Chiesa (Republican) and Lazzari (Socialist Maximalist).

[47] *Corriere della Sera*, 11–12 July (1923).

even smaller: 223 for and 123 against. Amendola voted against this time, together with the Socialists and Communists.

The electoral law reform significantly altered Italian constituencies, consolidating them from forty to fifteen, in addition to establishing a single national constituency. A maximum of two-thirds of the deputies allocated for each constituency could be candidates. The new law introduced the 'state ballot', printed by the Ministry of the Interior, with all the countersigns already indicated, which replaced the free ballot. Once the election was over, each polling station counted the votes and drew up the minutes, one of which was then sent to the Court of Appeal in Rome. At the Court of Appeal in Rome, the central office was set up, which added up all the votes obtained by the individual lists in the kingdom and checked which list had reached 25 per cent of the valid votes in the national college. It then allocated two-thirds of the deputies to this list and proclaimed all the candidates on the list elected in each constituency.

To determine the number of minority deputies, on the other hand, the votes of all the lists except the majority list were added together and this quotient was divided by the number of deputies to be elected (minority quotient).[48] On average, a deputy from the majority would be elected with a range between 7,600 votes in Sardinia and almost 10,000 in Piedmont (Table 7). A deputy from the minority, on the other hand, needed, on average, 50,000 votes to enter the chamber. For minority lists, the D'Hondt counting system introduced a further element of disproportionality, which decreased as the number of representatives to be elected in each constituency increased. Table 7 shows the distribution of seats and the size of the constituencies, which varied greatly, from the four minority deputies to be elected in Sardinia to the twenty-three in Lombardy.

The Construction of the Listone

On 25 January 1924, King Victor Emmanuel III signed the decree dissolving the chamber and called political elections for 6 April. The so-called Listone, or National Lists, comprising candidates aligned with the government, did not function as a typical party list but rather as a 'national force'. It broadened the candidate pool to include not only Fascists but also many others who, although not Fascists, endorsed the party's principles. Given the single national constituency, any list that did not present itself in all the constituencies wasn't seen as a real threat since, *ipso facto*, it could not take part in the challenge for the majority prize. Therefore, the presence of many liberal lists running outside the Listone did not indicate opposition to it, as they often maintained an ambiguous

---

[48] Articles 57–84 and 84a, 'Legge 18 Novembre 1923, n. 2444,' *Gazzetta Ufficiale del Regno d'Italia*, 3 December (1923).

Table 7 Key features of the Acerbo electoral law.

Constituency	Electorate	Total deputies	Majority list	Minority lists	Electorate per majority deputy	Electorate per minority deputy
Piedmont	1,197,561	47	31	16	9,658	56,136
Liguria	429,601	18	12	6	8,950	53,700
Lombardy	1,542,651	70	47	23	8,206	50,304
Veneto	1,109,602	53	35	18	7,926	46,233
New provinces	469,272	23	15	8	7,821	43,994
Emilia	921,996	41	27	14	8,537	49,393
Tuscany	904,824	38	25	13	9,048	52,201
Marche	378,613	16	11	5	8,605	56,792
Lazio and Umbria	669,469	30	20	10	8,368	50,210
Abruzzo and Molise	519,603	21	14	7	9,279	55,672
Campania	1,102,598	49	33	16	8,353	51,684
Apulia	662,011	32	21	11	7,881	45,137
Calabria and Basilicata	645,430	28	19	9	8,493	53,786
Sicily	1,270,334	57	38	19	8,357	50,145
Sardinia	245,771	12	8	4	7,680	46,082
Total	**12,069,336**	**535**	**356**	**179**	**8,476**	**50,570**

stance. None were candidates in all constituencies. Some, like Amendola, recognised the dangers of fragmentation and believed that the liberal opposition required a more robust organisation. A central issue among liberals at the time, one that would repeatedly resurface in the months that followed, was the normalisation of Fascism. Figures such as Croce downplayed the anxieties of those who feared an authoritarian turn.[49]

On the other hand, Mussolini had to fight internally within his party to prevent dissent. It was a fundamental moment because, in essence, the future Duce made it clear then that the fascists of the first hour had no right of pre-emption over those who came later. And so, too, the question of purism was to be viewed with suspicion.[50] It was clear that a 'Listone', in which many of the liberal notables had found a place, had not been digested. Mussolini himself was aware of the crucial nature of the moment, which is why he set up a group of five experienced people, the so-called 'pentarchy' formed by Rossi, Bianchi, Francesco Giunta, Acerbo, and Aldo Finzi, whose task it was to select the list of candidates from a group of 3,000 people. Mussolini's aim was to present himself as a man above the parties, linked to the PNF, but also capable of integrating part of the liberal world. For this, the pentarchy worked closely with Mussolini, not only with prefects and mayors but also with other members of local formations and parties (Rossi, 1958: 183). In February 1924, the work of the pentarchy was completed, and a list of 356 candidates was presented. This entire process must be encompassed within a continuous line from 1911, when the Libyan war erupted, to 1924. During this period, secular right-wing groups, clerical moderates, nationalists, futurists, and revolutionary syndicalists worked towards a tendentially organic state. It was a heterogeneous and contradictory group that grew stronger and stronger in those years without finding a defined form. This shape was finally given to it by Mussolini, whom we can define as a sort of right-wing federator.

To proceed to a deeper analysis of the prosopography of the deputies and to better understand the nature of the Listone, an attempt was made to collect the political elements of each of them. For a more precise analysis, it was decided to add to those in the Listone those elected in the 'Listone bis' (Nazionale bis);[51] that is, a list presented in those regions where fascism was strong enough to be able to think of recovering representatives even in the regional constituency. As we have seen, the Listone was not a fascist list *tout court*. Therefore, it is necessary to understand empirically which party families revolved around it. The criteria that were demanded of future candidates to be put on the list were

---

[49] Interview with Croce reported by *Corriere della Sera*, 1 February (1924).
[50] *Corriere della Sera*, 28 January, 1924.
[51] The Listone bis was presented in Tuscany, Lazio Umbria, Abruzzi, and Molise and Apulia.

Rise of Mass Parties, Liberal Italy, and Fascist Dawn (1919–1924) 65

generic, and in essence, the choice was somewhere between the old logic of blocs and the centralised control typical of the mass party. However, neither was the logic of the pre-electoral alliances, aggregations of more or less fluid parties that ceased to exist after the elections, as had been the case, for example, with the National Bloc of 1921, which dissolved when the traditional groups were reconstituted in the chamber.

In conducting this analysis, we have set ourselves objectives that differ from those pursued by others who have examined this data in the past. For example, Didier Musiedlak (2003) focused on establishing how many PNF members there actually were at the time of their candidature. Rossi (1965), who had been a member of the pentarchy, had instead limited himself to drawing up the list, specifying who was or was not a member of the PNF. Here, we will try to understand the deeper nature of the 'Amalgam-List', highlighting, for the fascists, the political formation of each of them before them joining fascism. The starting point from which we constructed the dataset was Rossi's list, but his data was meticulously cross-referenced and verified; an operation that might appear relatively easy, since we have at our disposal the historical archives of the Chamber of Deputies, numerous biographies that have been published in the meantime and the data from previous elections since 1919 indicating the candidate's party affiliation. Moreover, fascism, as we have repeatedly pointed out, had developed greatly in some areas of the country, namely those with a strong socialist structure, such as Emilia and Tuscany, but others had remained substantially impermeable. There is a notable distinction between the south and the north, where in the south, the fascist phenomenon was decidedly less deeply rooted and in which the prefects then played the very important role of managing the passage of the notability from one allegiance to another (Saija, 2001, p. 445). The pentarchy had in fact also had to select for the Listone a whole series of local notables to act as the transmission belt of fascism between the north, the centre and, above all, the south. And these were often little-known and scarcely traceable figures.

Unlike other analyses, we have categorised Nationalists as a separate entity. For while it is true that the unification between the PNF and Nationalists took place before the 1924 elections, it is equally true that, if we did not take this dimension into account, we would lose interesting data for interpreting what would later be the Chamber of Deputies and the context in which the battle for democracy, for some, and for dictatorship, for others, would develop. Among the names on the list, we categorised former members of the Popular Party, as well as figures from the liberal world, such as Orlando, Salandra, Alberto Giovannini, and the previously mentioned De Nava and De Nicola. The Listone is, therefore, a complex world that must be interpreted, from which the fluidity of the period can be perceived. It was far from being a cohesive and organic group. Nor was it organic to Mussolini, who nonetheless needed at the time to build a ruling class that was not made up only of thirty-year-olds with no political past and, therefore, found himself forced to look elsewhere for new figures.

The first dimension we considered was the party background of the Listone candidates and those elected from Listone bis, according to their initial political party affiliation. Table 8 shows the candidates derived from the four leading families that made up the Listone and Listone bis and by region. The first evidence is that Fascists without any other known political affiliation or past membership in other groups accounted for 56 per cent of the total. They were most numerous in regions such as Tuscany, Emilia, and Veneto, where the action squads had been strongest, but they were also present in regions like Liguria, Abruzzo, and Molise. On the opposite side, the regions where the Fascists had the least presence (below 50 per cent) were Piedmont, Sicily, Campania, and Marche.

The second dimension is the average age of the elected candidates divided by their political background. In this case (Table 9), for a more complete and effective comparison, we considered all the deputies elected to the chamber in 1924. The *Costituzionali*, whether elected in Listone or in other formations, form a single category, since no different average age was detected between the two groups. The deputies whose first political affiliation is with the PNF, with an average age of thirty-seven years, are by far the youngest among all political groups, followed, at some distance, by the Communists (with an average age of forty-one years). The highest average age was found among the reformist Socialists, averaging around fifty-one years.

In the third dimension, we considered the percentage of deputies belonging to the generation called upon to fight in the war, namely those born between 1874 and 1899 (Table 10). In this case, the comparison was made with the general percentage of all elected deputies. From Listone and Listone bis, divided between fascists and non-fascists, and finally, of deputies not elected within Listone and Listone bis. Table 10 shows that the war generation is decidedly predominant, with more than 70 per cent of all deputies. Within this group, 36 per cent were fascists and 19 per cent were equally divided among the other elected members of Listone and Listone bis, and those not elected on the government lists.

The fourth and final dimension: deputies elected for the first time in the 1924 elections. Table 11 highlights that the renewal rate is very high, at 55 per cent, but within this group, those elected whose first affiliation is with the PNF are the predominant part, comprising 33 per cent of all deputies experiencing their first term. To conclude, the data show that there is a very strong generational

Table 8 Members by political background of the 'Listone' and elected in the 'Listone bis'.

Region	Fascist		Nationalist		Popular Party		Costituzionali		Total
	N.	%	N.	%	N.	%	N.	%	N.
Piedmont	15	48.4%	2	6.5%	0	0.0%	14	45.2%	31
Liguria	8	66.7%	0	0.0%	0	0.0%	4	33.3%	12
Lombardy	27	57.4%	4	8.5%	3	6.4%	13	27.7%	47
Veneto	24	68.6%	0	0.0%	1	2.9%	10	28.6%	35
New provinces	10	66.7%	1	6.7%	0	0.0%	4	26.7%	15
Emilia	18	66.7%	2	7.4%	1	3.7%	6	22.2%	27
Tuscany	23	76.7%	1	3.3%	0	0.0%	6	20.0%	30
Marche	5	45.5%	1	9.1%	1	9.1%	4	36.4%	11
Lazio and Umbria	12	52.2%	2	8.7%	2	8.7%	7	30.4%	23
Abruzzo and Molise	14	73.7%	1	5.3%	0	0.0%	4	21.1%	19
Campania	12	37.5%	0	0.0%	3	9.4%	17	53.1%	32
Apulia	14	45.2%	0	0.0%	0	0.0%	17	54.8%	31
Calabria and Basilicata	10	52.6%	1	5.3%	2	10.5%	6	31.6%	19
Sicily	14	36.8%	2	5.3%	1	2.6%	21	55.3%	38
Sardinia	5	62.5%	0	0.0%	0	0.0%	3	37.5%	8
Total	**211**	**55.8%**	**17**	**4.5%**	**14**	**3.7%**	**136**	**36.0%**	**378**

Table 9 Average age of deputies at the time of their election in 1924, categorised by political background.

Region	Fascist	Nationalist	Socialist	Social Reformist	Communist	Popular	Costitutional
Piemonte	40.07	45	35	49.67	48.5	42	49.92
Liguria	36.25			59.5	51	36	55.25
Lombardia	35.74	43.5	48.4	58.25	38.5	50.18	49.08
Veneto	38.58		49	50.67	33	41.5	48.44
Venezia Giulia	40.11	37		46	43.5	46	53.75
Emilia	36.5	54	55.5	60	35	36.6	50.75
Toscana	34.96	43	37	47.5	30	37.5	45.2
Marche	37.4	33	40	50	29	41.5	58.33
Lazio e Umbria	33.25	46.5	36	46	46	39.75	49.4
Abruzzi e Molise	38	35		46			49
Campania	38		43	51	57	44.8	49.28
Puglie	36.21				46		47.38
Calabrie e Basilicata	38.4	46	47	32	36	57.25	49.27
Sicilia	41.43	39.5	38	44	52	43	48.71
Sardegna	34.8					47	33
Total	**37.24**	**43.41**	**44.2**	**51.79**	**41.58**	**44.5**	**49.21**

Table 10 Percentage of deputies born between 1874 and 1899, by political affiliation.

Region	Listone Fascist	Listone Other	Remaining deputies elected	Deputies elected (sum)
Piemonte	29.8%	19.1%	21.3%	70.2%
Liguria	38.9%	5.6%	5.6%	50.0%
Lombardia	38.6%	12.9%	17.1%	68.6%
Veneto	42.6%	11.1%	24.1%	77.8%
Venezia Giulia	34.8%	17.4%	30.4%	82.6%
Emilia	36.6%	12.2%	24.4%	73.2%
Toscana	61.5%	12.8%	17.9%	92.3%
Marche	25.0%	18.8%	25.0%	68.8%
Lazio e Umbria	38.7%	29.0%	22.6%	90.3%
Abruzzi e Molise	52.4%	19.0%	4.8%	76.2%
Campania	22.0%	22.0%	18.0%	62.0%
Puglie	42.4%	39.4%	3.0%	84.8%
Calabrie e Basilicata	30.0%	13.3%	23.3%	66.7%
Sicilia	21.1%	29.8%	15.8%	66.7%
Sardegna	41.7%	16.7%	33.3%	91.7%
Total	**36.2%**	**18.8%**	**18.8%**	**73.8%**

Table 11 Members of parliament elected to the chamber for the first time in 1924.

Region	Listone Fascist	Listone Other	Remaining MPs	All MPs (sum)
Piemonte	27.7%	14.9%	6.4%	48.9%
Liguria	44.4%	11.1%	0.0%	55.6%
Lombardia	31.4%	12.9%	5.7%	50.0%
Veneto	37.0%	7.4%	11.1%	55.6%
Venezia Giulia	26.1%	17.4%	17.4%	60.9%
Emilia	31.7%	14.6%	9.8%	56.1%
Toscana	48.7%	5.1%	5.1%	59.0%
Marche	25.0%	12.5%	12.5%	50.0%
Lazio e Umbria	35.5%	9.7%	3.2%	48.4%
Abruzzi e Molise	57.1%	4.8%	4.8%	66.7%
Campania	24.0%	16.0%	10.0%	50.0%
Puglie	39.4%	36.4%	6.1%	81.8%
Calabrie e Basilicata	33.3%	3.3%	13.3%	50.0%
Sicilia	24.6%	14.0%	1.8%	40.4%
Sardegna	41.7%	16.7%	16.7%	75.0%
Total	**33.6%**	**13.1%**	**7.6%**	**55.4%**

dynamic, a cohort effect of the fascist group that distinguishes them from deputies with a background in other parties. On one hand, it is certainly tautological to say that younger people fought in the trenches and were elected for the first time; on the other hand, however, it reveals an impressive group cohesion. In some ways, this makes this group similar to the elected members of the Communist Party.

The 1924 Elections

The elections of 1924 must be interpreted as a hybrid, in which the end of liberal Italy, the definitive end of the democratisation process and the still long and partly uncertain transition process towards the formalisation of dictatorship overlap. However, it is clear from the pages of the *Corriere della Sera* that, at the time, everyone, more or less, were resigned to the fact that the government list would be the winner. Given the state of prostration of the opposition, the meticulous control of the territory exercised by the Ministry of the Interior through the prefectural network and the control over the press, there could be no doubt about this. In such a scenario, the election campaign immediately became a plebiscite for or against the government.

Fascism emerged from the 1919–23 period profoundly reconfigured, something radically different from its beginnings. The opposition was divided into three camps: the 'class' opposition, Unitary Socialists, maximalists, and communists; the democratic opposition of Amendola and Bonomi; and the members of the Popular Party. The Liberals had been partly absorbed into the government forces, partly neutralised and, at least as far as Amendola and Bonomi's opposition was concerned, they had not yet fully grasped what was happening and how important it was to give themselves a structured organisation. Almost all of the liberal world of the constitutional parties had to varying degrees allowed themselves to be involved in fascism, between those who openly accepted a place in the Listone and those who indirectly ran for office in parallel lists such as Giolitti's (De Rosa, 1972: 278), which continued to support the government anyway. The Popular Party had split in the summer of 1923, after a long period of internal conflict that had seen the Sturzians and Grosoli's group opposed. They therefore participated with a national list, present in all fifteen constituencies. In essence, there was a shift from the formula 'neither opposition nor collaboration' to principled opposition, even if an anti-fascist opposition was not yet configured (Colarizi, 1973: 31). All attempts to build new political forces in the opposition camp with which to compete with the Listone fell on deaf ears: the attempt to reunite Amendola with Turati's '*Socialisti Unitari*' failed; Amendola's attempt to build constitutional opposition groups distributed throughout the country failed. Obviously weighing on these dynamics was a whole trail of suspicions and mistrust inherited from past positions. Thus, a tense climate reigned on the eve of the elections, with the knowledge that these elections would be much more violent than previous ones – something that was clear to everyone if only by unequivocal signs, such as the fact that part of the protection of public order had been attributed to the fascist militia.[52] King Vittorio Emanuele III once again offered his support to Mussolini on two notable occasions, both occurring during the month-long election campaign. On 18 March, Mussolini was awarded the Collar of the *Annunziata*, the highest honour the House of Savoy bestowed. Very few had and could receive it: in total, only twenty-two other Italians and among them only twelve politicians (including Giolitti, Salandra, and Leonida Bissolati). The main event of the whole campaign was the fascist gathering on 23 March to celebrate the fifth anniversary of the founding of the Fasci di Combattimento. The 2,000 Fascist mayors were summoned to Rome for a grand parade that marched first to commemorate the unknown soldier and then to pay homage to the Quirinale. It was in this context that the second episode occurred through which the monarchy clearly demonstrated its support for the Listone designed by Mussolini. The homage to the king and after that to the unknown soldier followed the events of 31 October 1922, and was clearly configured as a mutual recognition of the monarchy for the new government and of the fascists for the monarchy – a recognition that guaranteed the support of the conservative classes for fascism, especially in the south. It is important to emphasise the liturgy of the event which, on the one hand, took the form of homage to the king while, on the other hand, as a tribute to the square by the king who, for an hour and a half, remained in place to greet the passing cortege. In Mussolini's speech on that occasion, the link that the leader of fascism established between religion, the state, the union between classes and fascist doctrine deserves to be emphasised.

In addition to the king's intervention, the push for normalisation was further echoed in the speeches of prominent political figures from the Listone. For example, Salandra's address seamlessly intertwined the monarchy, the constitution, and Mussolini's government into a unified conceptual framework. Orlando was also in Salandra's line, who, on 3 April, from Palermo, returned to reasoning on the crisis of the state – the theme that had been raised at the turn of the century and that had nagged the conservative liberals.

The central theme of fascist propaganda during that campaign was the maintenance of the constitutional order. From their perspective, this order was

---

[52] *Corriere della Sera*, 6 March (1924).

threatened by the parliamentarist drift and the disruption caused by the 1919 elections. These elections, they argued, stemmed from a break in the state's organic unity due to the proportional electoral law. Organic unity was restored thanks only to the fascist government. By framing this narrative, Fascism transformed from a subversive force, as it appeared during the 1919 Piazza San Sepolcro meeting, into the agent of national and state restoration. It positioned itself as capable of reinstating authority and re-sacralising the homeland.

Election Results

The aforementioned factors played their part in election day. Even though the criteria for analysing this round cannot be those used for free and competitive elections, the results still provide important information.

First of all, participation in the ballot was very high (Table 12). Following a trend already seen in previous rounds, the number of voters grew again: it was just over seven million. Also changing radically were the participation rates, which had different trends from region to region and, therefore, need to be analysed one by one. There were many reasons for the growth in the vote, but they can basically be summed up by two: the violence and the strong consensus among the middle classes, who had finally found a force to represent them; the Listone. Also reinforcing this hypothesis were the results of the recent local elections. In fact, we had seen how the logic of bipolar and strongly ideologised confrontation between two different classes – on one side the socialists and, on the other, the organisations of shopkeepers and public employees – had given rise to a considerable increase in participation rates compared to the previous legislative elections. The further one went southwards, the more participation grew: Campania, Calabria, Basilicata, and Sardinia with a growth of around 10 per cent and Apulia, which was the region with the greatest anomalies and where participation grew by 28 per cent to 80 per cent. Conversely, in the north, participation fell, with the borderline case of Piedmont (–9 per cent of voters), or remained stable. If one then compares the participation figures with voting behaviour, a dynamic is evident in which most of the people who did not go to the polling stations were socialist voters.

There are two lines of analysis: one is the majority -opposition relationship, the other concerns the balances within the majority that we have already discussed in part. The Listone (Table 13) obtained a very high affirmation in general "(Listone 60.1%, Listone bis 4.8%, Total 64.9%) and its results followed the trends of participation: where it grew, so did the vote for the Listone. This also confirmed what had already happened in the local elections held

Table 12 Results of the 1924 Italian parliamentary elections.

Region	N. Lists	Newly elected MPs	Re-elected MPs	Newly elected (%)	Electorate	Voters	Emigrants	Soldiers	Valid votes	Voters (%)	Voters (1921–4)
Piedmont	9	23	24	48.94%	1,197,561	645,000	37,662	9,908	590,429	51.3%	−9.0%
Liguria	8	10	8	55.56%	429,601	252,702	8,861	5,742	236,198	56.9%	−1.1%
Lombardy	9	35	35	50.00%	1,542,651	1,112,002	27,097	11,250	1,023,978	68.1%	−3.6%
Veneto	8	32	21	60.38%	1,109,602	716,537	36,001	14,680	661,337	62.5%	−6.1%
New provinces	8	15	8	65.22%	469,272	287,949	17,300	8,637	268,325	60.5%	0.0%
Emilia	7	24	16	60.00%	921,996	682,024	14,672	9,358	640,367	71.3%	4.5%
Tuscany	9	21	17	55.26%	904,824	651,322	25,860	9,863	603,052	69.4%	3.7%
Marche	6	8	8	50.00%	378,613	217,029	25,521	9,968	202,043	58.9%	3.4%
Lazio and Umbria	11	15	14	51.72%	669,469	404,339	12,500	8,277	377,753	58.2%	2.8%
Abruzzo and Molise	7	13	8	61.90%	519,603	280,426	71,101	3,548	270,828	60.9%	4.2%
Campania	12	25	23	52.08%	1,102,598	620,777	90,938	9,078	599,544	59.8%	9.2%
Apulia	9	26	6	81.25%	662,011	533,384	26,334	8,035	526,415	83.9%	28.1%
Calabria and Basilicata	12	15	13	53.57%	645,430	357,171	96,260	4,965	345,788	63.5%	8.2%
Sicily	12	23	33	41.07%	1,270,334	707,038	92,391	10,666	680,860	58.3%	10.4%
Sardinia	6	9	3	75.00%	245,771	145,851	4,585	5,909	138,585	58.9%	6.3%
Total		294	237	55.37%	12,069,336	7,614,451	587,083	129,884	7,165,502	63.8%	3.1%

Table 13 Results of the 1924 Italian parliamentary elections (parties).

Region	Listone N.	Listone %	Listone Bis N.	Listone Bis %	Sum (proletarian parties) N.	Sum %	Sum (1921–4)	Popular Party N.	Popular Party %	Popular Party (1921–4)	Other Costituzionali N.	Other Costituzionali %	Fascista dissidente N.	Fascista dissidente %
Piedmont	265,823	45.0%			131,069	22.2%	–18.4%	62,661	10.6%	–11.4%	125,986	21.3%	4,890	0.8%
Liguria	123,633	52.3%			62,579	26.5%	–5.7%	30,521	12.9%	–11.0%	19,465	8.2%		
Lombardy	504,048	49.2%			301,866	29.5%	–16.6%	175,373	17.1%	–8.5%	29,519	2.9%	13,172	1.3%
Veneto	301,321	45.6%			136,788	20.7%	–9.9%	151,391	22.9%	–12.9%	71,837	10.9%		
New provinces	161,826	60.3%			38,968	14.5%	–14.0%	22,198	8.3%	–10.4%	45,333	16.9%		
Emilia	459,154	71.7%			100,816	15.7%	–22.9%	51,230	8.0%	–11.3%	29,167	4.6%		
Tuscany	390,672	64.8%	75,484	12.5%	71,524	11.9%	–29.8%	32,882	5.5%	–13.4%	32,490	5.4%		
Marche	128,869	63.8%			35,788	17.7%	–7.7%	21,253	10.5%	–19.3%	16,133	8.0%		
Lazio and Umbria	250,045	66.2%	36,544	9.7%	47,636	12.6%	–14.8%	20,005	5.3%	–14.4%	23,523	6.2%		
Abruzzo and Molise	150,906	55.7%	81,680	30.2%	15,857	5.9%	–4.1%	4,574	1.7%	–7.2%	17,811	6.6%		
Campania	457,740	76.3%			36,515	6.1%	–5.9%	20,187	3.4%	–11.9%	85,102	14.2%		
Apulia	286,612	54.4%	153,844	29.2%	15,170	2.9%	–17.4%	3,566	0.7%	–9.4%	67,223	12.8%		
Calabria and Basilicata	264,553	76.5%			18,218	5.3%	–5.5%	11,471	3.3%	–11.5%	51,546	14.9%		
Sicily	475,495	69.8%			33,249	4.9%	–3.4%	30,764	4.5%	–8.7%	141,343	20.8%		
Sardinia	85,239	61.5%			5,799	4.2%	–8.4%	7,713	5.6%	–5.8%	39,834	28.7%		
Total	4,305,936	60.1%	347,552		1,051,842	14.7%	–14.7%	645,789	9.0%	–11.4%	796,312	11.1%	18,062	0.3%

between 1922 and 1923. Similar to those rounds, the Listone proved to be strong in the regions where action squads had been very active (Emilia, Tuscany) and those in which the control over the constituencies by the prefects was more intense, that is, in the southern regions (Calabria and Basilicata, Campania, and Sicily, where it reached around 70 per cent). In Abruzzo Molise and Puglia, the Listone bis also obtained a very high result (around 30 per cent) which, added to the results of the Listone, brought the two 'government' lists to 80 per cent. In the north, conversely, it remained relatively weak: in Piedmont, Liguria, Lombardy, and Veneto it remained below or around 50 per cent. The three forces born from the Socialist Party (united socialists, maximalists, and communists) lost almost 15 per cent of the vote overall, with nearly 30 per cent in Tuscany, 22 per cent in Emilia and 18 per cent in Piedmont. The Popular Party managed to garner around 9 per cent overall (−11.4 per cent), ranging from 10 per cent in Piedmont to 23 per cent in Veneto. Finally, there was the fourth bloc, the Liberal Democrats, some of whom would end up some in the opposition and others in the government area, but who represented a relatively large part of the chamber that would be formed in 1924. The constitutional lists outside the Listone added up to almost 30 per cent in Sardinia and 20 per cent in Sicily. In essence, Italy remained divided in two, as it had been in all previous elections.

At first glance from Table 14, deputies elected with Fascist affiliation at the time of the 1924 election form by far the largest group. The national average for the Fascist Party's representation was 52.61%, demonstrating a dominant, though regionally variable, influence. Regions where this group was strongest include Tuscany (71.05%), Abruzzo and Molise (80.95%), and Apulia (66.67%), indicating significant regional support. Returning to our earlier analysis of the composition of the Listone, if we look at the results on the basis of the political background of the elected deputies, a picture is formed that confirmed some aspects that had already emerged, especially in the south, where there were many deputies with a liberal background (Table 14). There was a strong component of notables ferried into parliament – a phenomenon that becomes even more evident when comparing the data of all elected deputies, rather than limiting the analysis to those from the Listone and the Nazionale. The groups can be summarised in five macro-families: the fascist group (the largest but not the majority with 39.2 per cent); the constitutional deputies (25.3 per cent inside the list and 10.4 per cent outside the list), who formed the second largest group (overall 35 per cent); the class opposition (unitarians, maximalists, and communists), which suffered the greatest reduction, stopping at 12 per cent; the Catholics, divided between those who were members of the list (2.6%) and those who remained outside (7.2 per cent), remaining stable at 10 per cent) and finally the nationalists, always a very elitist formation, which corresponded

Table 14 Percentage and number of deputies by political party.

Region	Sum (proletarian parties)		Popular Party		Costituzionali (outside the Listone)		Fascist		Nationalist		Costituzionali (Listone)		Popular (Listone)		Total
	N.	%	N.	%	N.	%	N.	%	N.	%	N.	%	N.	%	N.
Piedmont	7	14.9%	3	6.4%	6	12.8%	15	31.9%	2	4.3%	14	29.8%			47
Liguria	3	16.7%	2	11.1%	1	5.6%	8	44.4%	0	0.0%	4	22.2%			18
Lombardy	13	18.8%	8	11.6%	1	1.4%	27	39.1%	4	5.8%	13	18.8%	3	4.3%	69
Veneto	7	13.2%	8	15.1%	3	5.7%	24	45.3%	0	0.0%	10	18.9%	1	1.9%	53
New Provinces	3	13.0%	2	8.7%	3	13.0%	10	43.5%	1	4.3%	4	17.4%			23
Emilia	8	19.5%	4	9.8%	2	4.9%	18	43.9%	2	4.9%	6	14.6%	1	2.4%	41
Tuscany	5	13.2%	2	5.3%	1	2.6%	23	60.5%	1	2.6%	6	15.8%			38
Marche	3	18.8%	1	6.3%	1	6.3%	5	31.3%	1	6.3%	4	25.0%	1	6.3%	16
Lazio and Umbria	4	13.3%	2	6.7%	1	3.3%	12	40.0%	2	6.7%	7	23.3%	2	6.7%	30
Abruzzo and Molise	1	4.8%	0	0.0%	1	4.8%	14	66.7%	1	4.8%	4	19.0%			21
Campania	4	8.3%	2	4.2%	10	20.8%	12	25.0%	0	0.0%	17	35.4%	3	6.3%	48
Apulia	1	2.8%	0	0.0%	4	11.1%	14	38.9%	0	0.0%	17	47.2%			36
Calabria and Basilicata	3	10.3%	1	3.4%	6	20.7%	10	34.5%	1	3.4%	6	20.7%	2	6.9%	29
Sicily	3	5.3%	3	5.3%	13	22.8%	14	24.6%	2	3.5%	21	36.8%	1	1.8%	57
Sardinia	0	0.0%	1	8.3%	3	25.0%	5	41.7%	0	0.0%	3	25.0%			12
Total	65	12.1%	39	7.2%	56	10.4%	211	39.2%	17	3.2%	136	25.3%	14	2.6%	538

Note: The total does not match the actual number of deputies because three elected members have resigned from their positions and have been replaced.

Rise of Mass Parties, Liberal Italy, and Fascist Dawn (1919–1924)   77

to 3 per cent. At the regional level there were very marked differences. In the south and in Piedmont the fascists were slightly weaker; in Campania and Sicily the fascist group was around 25 per cent and, in Emilia, Marche and Lombardy the socialist MPs made up almost 20 per cent. To this it must be added that the Senate, being non-elective, remained with a liberal majority.

In the summer of 1924, the Mussolini government trembled one last time, shaken by the case of the murder the sum of the proletarian MPs made up almost 20 per cent deputy Giacomo Matteotti by fascist squads. The Senate was then called upon to express confidence in the Mussolini government. It was not just a green light for the government but was a vote on the compatibility of fascism with liberal institutions, on its nature and on its ability to return the country to normalcy. Three-hundred-and-ninety senators voted in favour, there were no votes against and 142 abstained, a sign of a 'progressive integration of liberal circles into Fascism' (Musiedlak, 2003: 322). In the perception of the actors of the time, an alternative to Mussolini was possible, so much so that, as Musiedlak explains (2003: 320), there was even a rumour that Giolitti might lead a new government. Mussolini was aware of this and therefore asked for a vote of confidence in the Senate, hoping that it would be able to act as a buffer against possible opposition from the lower house, in a vote that was both a judgement on the government and on the nature of fascism. The operation succeeded, and the notables of liberalism, from Croce to Gaetano Mosca to Paolo Thaon di Revel, voted in favour of the confidence motion, thus implicitly recognising that fascism was compatible with the rule of law (Musiedlak, 2003: 323).

Conclusion

Italy had experienced a long period of democratisation that had begun in the very aftermath of the granting of the Albertine Statute in 1848 in what was still the Kingdom of Sardinia; a process that had intensified considerably, especially during the first two decades of the twentieth century. The key year was 1912, when universal male suffrage was approved. The entire political and party system felt the pressure of change and was deeply shaken by it. At the dawn of the new century, the Italian political scene thus found itself face to face, on the one hand, with an ever-growing Socialist Party – which stood as an open challenger to an entire hitherto dominant world – and, on the other, with a galaxy of conservative formations rooted in the old liberal order, which viewed with great distrust those masses of workers who, through parties and trade unions, had begun to question the established order. The expansion of mass parties was in fact a necessity of the times, the result of the change in society and the enlargement of suffrage, but it implied a totally different way of conceiving the relationship between parliament, the executive and the Crown.

The strong ideological charge that animated this type of party, the legitimacy that came to them from the breadth of their militant base and their rigid internal structures and organisation were all factors that greatly reduced their possibilities of mediation within parliament and in the relations between the three powers.

The first elections held under the new universal suffrage law in 1913 had not really resulted in very visible changes (Adinolfi, 2024). The uninominal constituency had allowed unorganised formations to concentrate the vote, including the Catholic one, on a specific candidate and in an anti-socialist function. The Socialist Party, although very strong in the northern regions, nevertheless had very little aggregative power over other formations that could concentrate the vote in the ballots compared to its opponents. After the First World War, this scenario changed completely. On the right, too, there began to be a need to organise in such a way as to be able to include the expanding middle classes in the state, just as the Socialists had done for the urban and agricultural proletariat. The first real experiment in this sense was the Fascio Parlamentare, a group that had sprung up in parliament – both in the Chamber of Deputies and the Senate – to support the government of Vittorio Emanuele Orlando in 1917, in the aftermath of the defeat at Caporetto in the First World War. With this experiment, an attempt was made to escape from the logic of the *notabilato* and to aggregate the liberal world on a national level, on the basis of a programme and hierarchy. However, the experiment failed as early as the summer of 1919, showing how little awareness the political actors in that area had of the radical nature of the transformations taking place. Catholics also organised themselves into a party: in 1919 the Popular Party was born. There were many lines in common with the Socialists, such as the grassroots organisation, made up of cooperatives, 'white unions' and sections. With the arrival of this new actor on the scene, the constitutional forces found themselves losing one of the pivots that had allowed them to stay alive, namely the Catholic vote which, in 1913, had still converged on 'ministerial' candidates: they saw the emergence of a competitor within their area decidedly more capable than them of organising consensus.

The real political turning point came with the elections of November 1919, which were held with the proportional electoral system on a constituency basis, a system that still did not fully reward the mass integration parties but allowed liberals like Giolitti, Salandra, or Orlando to run their constituencies like fiefdoms. If until then the political debate had been concerted on the need to complete the democratisation process in the country, as was happening in the rest of Europe (i.e., with a discussion on the two hypotheses of a constitutional assembly and reform of the Senate), the shock due to the impact of the great and unexpected affirmation of the Socialist and Popular Parties almost completely blocked this discussion. The Senate, by royal appointment, became the bastion of the defence of the liberal order in a system in which laws had to be passed by both branches of parliament. It meant the blocking of the functioning of the system. In the other chamber, in fact, transformations were bursting in force: only 39 per cent of the deputies were re-elected, but not only that, 50 per cent of the deputies were members of either the Popular Party or the Socialist Party. In order to adapt to the changed equilibrium and to conform to a new reality that was much less fluid than in the past, even the internal regulations of the Chamber of Deputies were revised, leaving the constitutional forces much less room for manoeuvre.

The cleavages were not only inter-party, but also intra-party, institutional, and geographical. In the north, the mass integration parties clearly dominated (the Socialists amassed 50 per cent of the deputies and the Popular Party 26 per cent) while, in the south, the mass parties were practically irrelevant (Socialists under 5 per cent and the Popular Party under 15 per cent). The Socialists were divided between a maximalist – and communist – wing and a reformist wing. The Popular Party was divided between an intransigent faction, whose aim was to continue the democratisation process by conquering and replacing the liberals, and a conservative wing, which was instead interested in allying itself with the liberals in an anti-socialist function, being determined to maintain the status quo. The world of the 'constitutional' parties was completely pulverised and blocked by the conflict that divided Giolitti and Salandra, but which was united in the objective of preventing the Socialists from growing and the Catholics from occupying their space, entrenched in the Senate and together with the Crown.

All these cleavages indelibly marked the local elections of 1920, which were held under a majoritarian electoral system. These elections were important for three reasons. Firstly, because the municipalities then had broad powers of intervention both in the sphere of the economy, taking space away from the private sector to create modern systems of public services, and in the sphere of taxation to finance these interventions. Secondly, because at this level, unlike at the national level, Socialists were not precluded from occupying executive positions. Finally, because they marked both the apogee of the democratisation process and the beginning of the reaction. It was easy for the liberals to propose large anti-socialist blocs on a local scale; it was difficult for the Popular Party to accept them and the Catholics split into two increasingly irreconcilable factions. The reformist Socialists faction in the Socialist Party, a minority, were not expelled, but they were essentially barred from any major role. The elections were a partial victory for the Socialists but, at the same time, they showed the anti-socialist forces that by fielding very broad aggregations and a highly polarising communication strategy it would be possible to mobilise the conservative electorate and secure unexpected victories, like the one in Turin, or narrow defeats, like the one in Milan. Where liberals and conservatives had been active with competitive lists, abstention fell by as much as twenty percentage points compared to the 1919 legislative elections. In this context, Benito Mussolini's Fasci di Combattimento had still been largely marginal. The turning point came with the storming of the Palazzo d'Accursio, the seat of Bologna's city hall, where the new council led by a maximalist Socialist, was to take office. It was only then that fascism, especially in Emilia, Tuscany, Lombardy, and Veneto, began to grow into a mass phenomenon.

In the political elections of 1921, which were held under the proportional system, part of the liberal world tried to organise large blocs at the national level, including the fascists, with a clear anti-socialist will. These blocs, far from being a party and having a coherent organisation, had instead presented themselves in each constituency with different names and combinations: the Liberals, while realising that the competition had changed, still hoped that a modest make-up operation might be sufficient to adapt to the new course. From this perspective, the 1921 elections were a debacle for the Liberals, who fielded candidates under almost 50 different acronyms, with each appearing in only an average of two constituencies. It was the fascists who took advantage of these weaknesses, and it was not difficult for them, being at that point the only nationally organised force, to assume the leadership of the right-wing camp. Not surprisingly, it was often the fascist candidate who gained the most preferences in individual constituencies. These results apparently did not change the structure of the party system very much, but in fact introduced the fascist movement into the conservative bloc, a formation that had managed to give itself a national structure in the meantime, which would later become the PNF and which, between 1920 and 1921, would move from its initial revolutionary positions to conservative ones.

By the time of the March on Rome, Mussolini was already arriving as one of the possible solutions to the collapse of liberal Italy which, moreover, was so unaware that it did not realise that fascism would not be a useful tool for defeating the Reds but would end up destroying the liberal order itself. To the presidency of the council, which came about in the aftermath of Facta's resignation – submitted before the March on Rome took place – and which saw all the 'Constitutional' forces plus the Popular Party united, Mussolini therefore did not arrive suddenly. The Fascist parliamentary group had long since organised itself with right-wing Liberals and Nationalists into an informal group in the chamber and was an active and accepted part of every electoral coalition. It had been taking part in consultations at the Quirinale with the king since 1921. And, above all, it had been negotiating for months for PNF entry into any government led by Salandra, Giolitti, or Orlando.

Once again, playing a periodising role were the administrative elections; those which took place between 1922 and 1923. It was, in fact, necessary to renew a large number of municipal councils, generally Socialist, that had been dissolved by the prefects following fascist violence. The PNF took part in this round for the first time, not as a gregarious participant, but as a protagonist in non-competitive elections in which the Liberals accepted to be subordinated to the new force of the nation. With a few exceptions, such as Milan, the Socialists did not even participate. The PNF won all those that had been 'Red' municipalities with both majority and minority lists. At the same time, parliament was debating the new electoral law for political elections, which was to remain known as the Acerbo Law, and would have awarded the party that obtained at least 25 per cent of the votes: a two-thirds majority of the seats at national level. It was a law made to allow an organised and hierarchical mass party win, because it provided for a single national constituency whose candidates were chosen by a top leadership. In the process of passing the electoral law, the deciding factor was the Popular Party: in the balance of parliamentary numbers, it was the Populars with their votes who decided whether this law could pass. And on this the Catholics split: the more conservative wing sided with Mussolini, the intransigent wing ended up abstaining. The Liberals, with different tones, were all in favour. The only ones against were the Socialists – who in the meantime had split into maximalists and reformists – and the Communists.

During the long process of discussion of the Acerbo Law there was also an underground process of negotiation between the PNF and the Liberals to set up a list, what would later become the *Listone*, for the 1924 elections in which part of the liberal world and the *notabilato* of the south, where fascism was still weak, would be channelled. In the Listone, the component that had a non-fascist political past would be very strong. Mussolini had managed to absorb all the conservative forces and hegemonise them. The Church, showing scepticism towards Don Sturzo, and even looking favourably on collaboration with the conservatives, had wrecked the Popolari and the Crown, a month before the elections, had sanctioned the normalisation of fascism by offering Mussolini the highest honour of the House of Savoy: the Collar of the *Annunziata*. Of the victory of the government list, no one had any doubts. The elections of 1924 can certainly not be considered competitive elections. However, this does not prevent us from emphasising that the mobilisation of the middle classes had been strong: at last, they, too, had a party that represented them. It is also in this scheme that Mussolini fits. Fascism, however, aligns with something pre-existing that can be traced back to the Italo-Turkish War of 1911–2, to the movements of university students and the birth of nationalism and then, clearly, to 1915 and the 'radiant May' that, partly violently, had forced parliament to vote in favour of Italy's entry into the war. Fascism integrated into all this, into the liberal and conservative world's fear of the threat of socialism and the organised labour movement, into the fear of the new Catholic world organised by the Popular Party and into traditional nationalism. To all this, however, fascism brought something special: the nationalisation of the middle classes and the hierarchical structure developed at national level.

The Liberals, who had aligned themselves with Mussolini hoping both to defeat the Socialists and to preserve Italy from the conquest of the mass parties, had essentially committed suicide by allowing the most organised and authoritarian of these to win (Sabbatucci, 1989: 57–80). The failure to set up a mass integration party of liberals, as the historian De Felice has brilliantly explained (1966: 41), was therefore one of the causes of the collapse of liberal Italy, which at first had tolerated the fascists and the awakening of the middle classes in an anti-socialist function, but soon fell victim to them. Italy failed in its appointment with democracy because an important slice of society did not recognise itself within it and did not do so because it lacked a party to which it could entrust itself (Farneti, 1978: 25–8). The inability of the liberals to understand that elitist politics structured on a proprietary view of the constituency was over and that the emerging middle classes also needed to be represented led to a disconnect between society and parliament.

References

Books, Journal Articles, and Chapters in Edited Books

Abisso, A. (1927). *Dal fascio parlamentare al Partito Nazionale Fascista*, Rome: Società Anonima Poligrafica Italiana.

Adinolfi, G. (2009). The Fascist Elites, Government and the Grand Council. *Portuguese Journal of Social Science*, 8(1), 7–30.

Adinolfi, G. (2022). Continuities and Discontinuities in the Processes of Elite Recruitment: The Italian Political Field between Authoritarianism and Democratic Regime. *Topoi*, 41, 79–92.

Adinolfi, G. (2024). Italy between Liberalism and Democracy: Universal Suffrage and the 1913 Elections. *Modern Italy*, 1–20. doi.org/10.1017/mit.2024.29.

Alatri, P. (1961). *Le origini del fascismo*, Rome: Editori Riuniti.

Albanese, G. (2008). *La marcia su Roma*, Rome, Bari: Laterza.

Albanese, G. (2016). *Dittature mediterranee. Sovversioni fasciste e colpi di Stato in Italia, Spagna e Portogallo*, Bari: Laterza.

Ambrosini, G. (1922). La trasformazione del regime parlamentare e del governo di gabinetto. *Rivista di diritto pubblico*, 14, 187–200.

Antonetti, N. (1985). Luigi Sturzo e il problema della rappresentanza parlamentare nella crisi dello stato liberale... *Il Politico*, 50(2), 253–73.

Arfé, G. (1975). *Storia del socialismo Italiano 1892–1926*, Turin: Einaudi.

Bachi, R. (1903). Un'inchiesta sulla municipalizzazione dei pubblici servizi in Italia. *Riforma sociale*, 10, 5–29.

Ballini, P. L. (2002). Le 'regole del gioco': dai banchetti elettorali alle campagne disciplinate. In P. L. Ballini and M. Ridolfi, eds., *Storia delle campagne elettorali in Italia*, Milan: Bruno Mondadori, pp. 1–64.

Ballini, P. L. (2011). *La questione elettorale in Italia, da Salandra a Mussolini (1914–1928)*, Rome: Camera dei Deputati.

Ballini, P. L., and Ridolfi, M. (2002). *Storia delle campagne elettorali in Italia*, Milan: Bruno Mondadori.

Baravelli, A. (2021). Un voto in grigioverde. Il tema della lezione della guerra nella campagna elettorale dell'autunno 1919. In G. Schinnà, ed., *Le elezioni del 1919. Alle origini del sistema politico dell'Italia contemporanea*, Milan: Le Monnier, pp. 212–378.

Belardinelli, M. (1979). *Movimento cattolico e questione comunale dopo l'Unità*, Rome: Studium.

Bidussa, D. (2022). La violenza fascista come pratica politica identitaria. In G. De Luna, ed., *Fascismo e storia d'Italia*, Milan: Feltrinelli, pp. 3–22.

Cantono, A. (1920). *Il programma del Partito Popolare Italiano*, Turin: Società Editrice Internazionale.

Colarizi, S. (1973). *I democratici all'opposizione, Giovanni Amendola e l'Unione nazionale (1922–1926)*, Bologna: Il Mulino.

Colombo, P. (2010). *La monarchia fascista 1922–1940*, Bologna: Il Mulino.

D'Amuri, M. (2013). *La casa per tutti nell'età giolittiana. Provvedimenti e iniziative per la municipalizzazione dell'edilizia popolare*, Milan: OpenEdition Books.

De Bernardi, A. (2022). 28 ottobre 1922. La marcia su Roma. La conquista. In S. Lupo, ed., *Il fascismo nella storia italiana*, Rome: Donzelli, pp. 65–82.

De Felice, R. (1965). *Mussolini il rivoluzionario (1883–1920)*, Turin: Einaudi.

De Felice, R. (1966). *Mussolini il fascista. La conquista del potere 1921–1925*, Turin: Einaudi.

De Maria C., ed. (2010). *Andrea Costa e il governo della città. L'esperienza amministrativa di Imola e il municipalismo popolare 1881–1914*, Reggio Emilia: Diabasis.

De Rosa, G. (1972). *Il partito popolare italiano*, Bari: Laterza.

Degl'Innocenti, M. (1984). Il comune nel socialismo italiano. 1892–1922. *Italia contemporanea*, 154, 5–28.

Duverger, M. (1954). *Political Parties: Their Organisation and Activity in the Modern State*, London: Methuen & Co.

Farneti, P. (1978). Social Conflict, Parliamentary Fragmentation, Institutional Shift, and the Rise of Fascism: Italy. In J. Linz and A. Stepan, eds., *The Breakdown of Democratic Regimes, Europe*, Baltimore: The Johns Hopkins University Press, pp. 3–31.

Flores, M., and Gozzini, G. (2022). *Perché il fascismo è nato in Italia*, Bari: Editori Laterza.

Frangioni, A. (2019). La Grande Guerra in Parlamento: l'Unione parlamentare e il Fascio parlamentare di difesa nazionale. In R. Pace, ed., *La fatalità della guerra e la volontà di vincerla: classe dirigente liberale, istituzioni e opinione pubblica*, Soveria Mannelli: Rubbettino, pp. 113–29.

Franzinelli, M. (2019). *Squadristi, Protagonisti e tecniche della violenza fascista 1919–1922*, Milan: Feltrinelli.

Gaeta, F. (1981). *Il Nazionalismo italiano*, Rome: Laterza.

Gentile, E. (2002). *Il mito dello Stato nuovo dall'antigiolittismo al fascismo*, Rome: Laterza.

Gentile, E. (2011). *Le origini dell'ideologia fascista 1918–1925*, Bologna: Il Mulino.

Gentile, E. (2014). *E fu subito regime. Il Fascismo e la Marcia su Roma*, Rome: Laterza.

Gentile, E. (2022). *Storia del fascismo*, Rome: Laterza.

Gentiloni Sivieri, U. (1999). *Conservatori senza partito. Un tentativo fallito nell'Italia giolittiana*, Rome: Edizioni Studium.

Giolitti, G. (1952). *Discorsi extra-parlamentari*, Turin: Einaudi.

Giovannini, E. (2001). *L'Italia massimalista, socialismo e lotta sociale e politica nel primo dopoguerra italiano*, Rome: Ediesse.

Giusti, U. (1922). *Le correnti politiche italiane attraverso due riforme elettorali dal 1909 al 1921*, Florence: Alfani & Venturi.

Giusti, U. (1945). *Dai plebisciti alla costituente*, Rome: Editrice Faro.

Gramsci, A. (1973). *Sul fascismo*, Rome: Editori Riuniti.

Grassi F., Quagliariello, G., and Orsina G., eds. (1996). *Il partito politico dalla grande guerra al fascismo*, Bologna: Il Mulino.

Lanciotti, M. E. (1993). *La riforma impossibile. Idee, discussioni e progetti sulla modifica del Senato regio e vitalizio 1848–1922*, Bologna: Il Mulino.

Leoni, F. (2001). *Storia dei partiti politici italiani*, Naples: Alfredo Guida Editore.

Lo Bue, M. (2019). *CIDIU, Un'azienda pubblica nel contesto dell'area metropolitana torinese*, Turin: Industrie Grafiche Falciola.

Mencarelli, P., ed. (2019). *Inchiesta socialista sulle gesta dei fascisti in Italia*, Milan: Biblion Edizioni.

Michels, R. (1949). *Partiti e sindacati nella crisi del regime parlamentare*, Bari: Laterza.

Montemartini, G. (1903). *La questione delle Case Operaie in Milano*. Milan: Editore l'Ufficio del lavoro.

Mosca, G. (1896). *Elementi di Scienza Politica*, Rome: Bocca.

Musiedlak, D. (2003). *Lo stato fascista e la sua classe politica 1922–1943*, Bologna: Il Mulino.

Musiedlak, D. (2022). *La marche sur Rome: entre histoire et mythe*, Paris: Sorbonne Université Presses.

Nardi, I., and Gentili, S. (2009). *La grande illusione: opinione pubblica e mass media al tempo della guerra di Libia*, Perugia: Morlacchi Editore.

Noiret, S. (1989). Riforme elettorali e crisi dello stato liberale, La 'Proporzionale' 1918–1919, *Italia Contemporanea*, 174, 29–56.

Offerlé, M. (1999). *La profession politique XIX–XX siècles*, Paris: Belin.

Orsina, G. (1996). L'organizzazione politica nelle Camere della proporzionale (1920–1924). In F. Grassi, G. Quagliariello, and G. Orsina, eds., *Il partito politico dalla grande guerra al fascismo*, Bologna: Il Mulino, pp. 397–492.

Peclone, F. (1983). *Novant'anni di pensiero e azione socialista attraverso i congressi del Psi, 1917–1937*, Vol. II, Venice: Marsilio Editori.

Perazzoli, J. (2022). *Angelo Filippetti, l'ultimo sindaco di Milano prima del fascismo*, Milan: Biblion Edizioni.

Pullé, F., and Vegliasco G. (1932). *Memorie del Fascio Parlamentare di difesa nazionale (Senato e Camera)*, Bologna: Cappelli.

Regno d'Italia (1889). *Testo unico della legge comunale e provinciale, approvato con R. Decreto 10 Febbraio 1889, n. 5921. Regolamento e disposizioni relative, con Indice alfabetico analitico*, Livorno: Raffaello.

Ridolfi, M. (1992). *Il Psi e la Nascita del partito di Massa 1892–1922*, Rome: Laterza.

Ridolfi, M. (2000). *Nel segno del voto, Elezioni, rappresentanza e culture politiche nell'Italia liberale*, Rome: Carocci Editore.

Rossi C. (1965). *Il delitto Matteotti nei procedimenti giudiziari e nelle polemiche giornalistiche*, Milan: Casa Editrice Ceschina.

Rossi, C. (1958). *Trentatré vicende mussoliniane*, Milan: Casa Editrice Ceschina.

Sabbatucci, G. (1980). I socialisti nella crisi dello Stato liberale 1918–1926. In *Storia del socialismo italiano, vol. III, Guerra e dopoguerra*, Rome: Il Poligono editore, pp. 135–404.

Sabbatucci, G. (1989). Il 'suicidio' della classe dirigente liberale. La legge Acerbo 1923–1924. *Italia Contemporanea*, 174, 57–80.

Saija, M. (2001). *I prefetti italiani nella crisi dello stato liberale*, Milan: Giuffré Editore, 2001.

Schiavi, A. (1911). *Le case a buon mercato e le città giardino*, Bologna: Zanichelli.

Schiavi, A. (1914). Le forze e i programmi dell'opposizione nell'ultima campagna elettorale politica, *La Riforma Sociale, Rivista critica di economia e di finanza*, 21(25), 413–75.

Spriano, P. (1967). *Storia del Partito Comunista Italiano, vol. I*, Turin: Einaudi.

Sturzo, L. (1956). Crisi e rinnovamento dello stato. In *Il Partito popolare italiano, vol. I*, Bologna: Zanichelli, pp. 264–5.

Tittoni, T. (1918). I conflitti tra le due Camere in Inghilterra e la riforma della Camera dei Lords – II – La crisi costituzionale. *Nuova Antologia*, 6(1123), 17–41.

Ullrich, H (1996). Dai gruppi al partito liberale 1919–1922. In F. Grassi, G. Quagliariello, and G. Orsina, eds., *Il partito politico dalla grande guerra al fascismo*, Bologna: Il Mulino, pp. 493–530.

Ventura, A. (2021). *Il diciannovismo fascista. Un mito che non passa*, Rome: Viella.

Visani, A. (2004). *La conquista delle maggioranza. Mussolini, il PNF e le elezioni del 1924*, Genova: Fratelli Frilli editori.

Journals and Newspapers

Avanti!
Corriere della Sera
Critica Sociale
Il Popolo d'Italia
Il Giornale d'Italia
La Stampa
Nuova Antologia
Riforma sociale

Electoral Statistics

Istituto Centrale di Statistica e Ministero per la Costituente (1946), *Elettori Politici e Circoscrizioni elettorali*. Vol. I of *Compendio delle Statistiche elettorali italiane dal 1848 al 1934*, Rome: Stabilimento Tipografico F. Failli.

Istituto Centrale di Statistica e Ministero per la Costituente (1947), *Frequenza alle urne – Candidati ed eletti – Partiti politici – Elezioni amministrative comunali e provinciali*, Vol. II of *Compendio delle Statistiche elettorali italiane dal 1848 al 1934*, Rome: Stabilimento Tipografico F. Failli.

Ministero dell'economia nazionale, Direzione Generale della Statistica (1924a). *Statistica delle elezioni generali politiche per la XXVI Legislatura (15 maggio 1921)*, Rome: Industrie Grafiche.

Ministero dell'economia nazionale, Direzione Generale della Statistica (1924b). *Statistica delle elezioni Generali Amministrative del 1920*, Rome: Industrie Grafiche.

Ministero dell'economia nazionale, Direzione Generale della Statistica (1924), *Statistica delle elezioni generali politiche per la XXVII Legislatura (6 aprile 1924)*, Rome: Libreria dello Stato.

Ministero di agricoltura, industria e commercio, Direzione generale della statistica e del lavoro (Ufficio centrale di statistica) (1914). *Statistica delle elezioni generali politiche per la XXIV Legislatura, (26 ottobre e 2 novembre 1913)*, Rome: Tipografia Nazionale di G. Bertero e C.

Ministero per l'Industria, il commercio ed il lavoro, Ufficio Centrale di Statistica (1920). *Statistica delle elezioni generali politiche per la XXV Legislatura, (16 Novembre 1919)*, Rome: Stabilimento Poligrafico per l'amministrazione della guerra.

Funding Statement

Research funded by Fundação para a Ciência e a Tecnologia, within the scope of the contract programme foreseen in the numbers 4, 5, and 6 of article 23 of Decree-Law n. 57/2016.

Cambridge Elements⹀

The History and Politics of Fascism

Series Editors
Federico Finchelstein
The New School for Social Research
Federico Finchelstein is Professor of History at the New School for Social Research and Eugene Lang College in New York City. He is an expert on fascism, populism, and dictatorship. His previous books include *From Fascism to Populism in History* and *A Brief History of Fascist Lies*.

António Costa Pinto
University of Lisbon
António Costa Pinto is a Research Professor at the Institute of Social Sciences, University of Lisbon. He is a specialist in fascism, authoritarian politics, and political elites. He is the author and editor of multiple books on fascism, including (with Federico Finchelstein) *Authoritarianism and Corporatism in Europe and Latin America*.

Advisory Board
Giulia Albanese, *University of Padova*
Mabel Berezin, *Cornell University*
Maggie Clinton, *Middlebury College*
Sandra McGee Deutsch, *University of Texas, El Paso*
Aristotle Kallis, *Keele University*
Sven Reichardt, *University of Konstanz*
Angelo Ventrone, *University of Macerata*

About the Series
Cambridge Elements in the History and Politics of Fascism is a series that provides a platform for cutting-edge comparative research in the field of fascism studies. With a broad theoretical, empirical, geographic, and temporal scope, it will cover all regions of the world, and most importantly, search for new and innovative perspectives.

Cambridge Elements

The History and Politics of Fascism

Elements in the Series

Populism and Fascism
Carlos de la Torre

The Rise of Mass Parties, Liberal Italy, and the Fascist Dawn (1919–1924)
Goffredo Adinolfi

A full series listing is available at: www.cambridge.org/CEHF

For EU product safety concerns, contact us at Calle de José Abascal, 56–1°, 28003 Madrid, Spain or eugpsr@cambridge.org.